THE RIGHT WAY
TO PLAY CHESS

THE RIGHT WAY
TO PLAY CHESS

(ILLUSTRATED)

by
D. BRINE PRITCHARD

PAPERFRONTS
ELLIOT RIGHT WAY BOOKS
KINGSWOOD, SURREY, U.K.

Made and printed in Great Britain by
C. Nicholls & Company Ltd.
and published by
Elliot Right Way Books
Kingswood Surrey U.K.

CONTENTS

INTRODUCTION

The Right Way to Play Chess has now served as tutor to a generation of readers and it is a continual source of satisfaction to me to be approached by young, and sometimes not-so-young experts and be told that their introduction to the game was through this book.

Chess is perennial but not changeless. Many developments have taken place in the game during the last twenty years and these have been reflected in succeeding editions of The Right Way to Play Chess. It may therefore comfort you to know that this book was right up to date at the time of going to Press and for practical purposes is likely to remain so for a few years at least, by which time, if past experience is to be relied on, it will be overtaken by a new edition.

Chess is not an easy game, but any idea that you have to be highly intelligent or "clever" to play it should be dismissed. If the game were easy to master, it would be trivial and would attract little interest. On the other hand, if chess were hard to learn it would not be played – and often played well – by six- and seven-year-olds. The magic of chess is that it can be learnt by almost anyone, played almost anywhere and at almost any level with equal enjoyment. One of my most enthusiastic correspondents, by no means an expert, is a retired nurse who, having come to the game late in life, has discovered in chess an interest that totally absorbs her, her one regret being that she did not know the game when she was younger.

The developments in the game over the past twenty years, to which I referred above, have been exciting ones. Chess has suddenly become both respectable and popular.

The World Championship match at Rekjavik in 1972 between Bobby Fischer and Boris Spassky attracted world-wide publicity, though admittedly for reasons not wholly to do with chess. This accelerated the boom which had started years before and which, against many predictions, has yet to show signs of a decline. Chess, it appears, is here to stay; not just as an indoor game but as a major field of intellectual activity with wide support from educationalists as well as the public at large.

Millions of people – literally – play at home in the family circle and with friends but never take the game seriously. At the other end of the spectrum there is a growing body of chess professionals, in Europe and the Americas in particular. In between these two groups are what may be called the club players who vary from the man who turns out occasionally for his works' team to the enthusiast who gives most of his spare time to the game and enters for every event in the calendar.

The standard of play, certainly at the higher levels and probably at the club level as well, has risen remarkably. Whereas thirty or so years ago the international scene was dominated by a handful of masters, now there is a small army of them and behind them another, larger army of players only marginally below master strength.

How has this come about? The explanation is easy to find: youth has taken the game for its own. If you look in to-day on almost any chess event you will be struck by the number of young players, many of school age, taking part. This phenomenon is the natural outcome of the rapid growth of chess clubs and chess teaching in schools that has taken place since the war. The image of chess as an old man's game has quietly died.

The World Olympiads – the Olympic Games of chess – are held regularly, each Olympiad bigger than the last as more and more countries are represented. Now one counts teams from Hong Kong, Guernsey, Andorra and the British Virgin Islands side by side with the giants and it becomes increasingly difficult to discern which countries are *not* represented. At the Olympiads, too, youth is very much in evidence.

At no period in its long history has the game been so intensely studied as at present. Recent researches have led to many theoretical advances, particularly in the opening phase (chess openings, since they begin from a standard position, lend themselves more readily to analysis than other stages of the game). Old ideas have been challenged, techniques perfected, styles modified, fashions changed.

Yet it is true to say that the basics of the game remain invariable and The Right Way to Play Chess is as relevant today as when it was first written. The book is planned to take the complete beginner to the standard expected of a good club player. The journey should be a pleasant one, for chess is above all a game and a game is to be enjoyed. A chess set is necessary to follow the text. A plain wooden or plastic set is best. The type known as Staunton pattern is the most widely used and is recommended.

The final chapter gives some general information for the reader who wishes to take the game seriously. It is necessarily brief, but hopefully provides sufficient insight into the exciting world of competitive chess to encourage further enquiry.

It would be wrong to leave this introduction without a brief mention of the history of the game. The precise origins of chess are obscure but it was almost certainly evolved from a four-handed game of ancient India known as chaturanga. From chaturanga was developed a two-player version, called shatranj, the true forerunner of our chess. The game reached Europe via Persia and the Arab lands by about the 9th century, and for many hundred years remained a pastime of the rich and privileged. Popular interest in the game spread as cheap printing made communication easier and technical advancements afforded greater leisure.

Over the centuries the rules of the game have benefited from many changes, and even to-day minor amendments are made from time to time for the game is still in evolution. But even with its slight imperfections chess remains for millions indisputably the best two-player game in the world. This is something that will not change.

D.B.P.

CHAPTER I
HOW THE GAME IS PLAYED

The Game

The game of chess is played between two players or parties on a board of sixty-four squares (8×8) alternately coloured light and dark (normally black and white).

Each player has at his command a force of sixteen men; *eight pieces* (one king, one queen, two rooks, two bishops, two knights) and *eight pawns*. The opposing forces are usually coloured, and are referred to as White and Black.

Players move in turn, and the object of the game is to capture (checkmate) the opposing king.

Each chessman is governed by its own rules of movement and is now examined separately.

The King (♔♚)

The king moves one square in any direction, but since he takes seven moves to cross the board he is a comparatively weak piece. However, the importance of the king is evident from the previous paragraph—his loss entails the loss of the game.

The king may not therefore be moved onto a square attacked by an opposing man. If the king is attacked (i.e., if he is *threatened with capture* on the next move), he is said to be "in check", and the opponent may, but is not obliged to say "check" when making the move that attacks the king.

The player whose king is threatened *must immediately*

move out of check.   There are three methods of doing this:

(1) By moving the king on to a square not attacked by an enemy man.

(2) By capturing the attacking unit, either with the king or with another man.

(3) By moving a man between the king and the attacker.

Not all these resources may be available.   If none are playable—that is, if the king has no square to which to

DIAGRAM 1

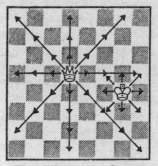

THE KING AND QUEEN

move out of check, the attacking man may not be captured and no man may be interposed—then the king is said to be " checkmated ", or, simply " mated ", and the game is over.   Note that the king is the only piece that can never *actually* be captured—the game is concluded on the imminence of the inevitable.

A king may capture an opposing man by moving on to the square on which it stands, simultaneously removing it from the board.   Since it is illegal for the king to move into check, only an undefended man may be so captured.

Capturing in chess is not compulsory (as in draughts), and there is no " huffing " or jumping over the captured man. The two kings must not stand on adjacent squares, since both would then be in check from one another.

The Queen (♛♛)

The queen moves in any direction across any number of squares that may be vacant. Her move is an extension of the king's move, limited only by the confines of the board. She is the most powerful of the pieces.

The queen captures in the same manner as the king, but since she is not liable to check, she may capture a man that is defended, although such a movement is unusual, as, being the most powerful piece, the queen is rarely surrendered voluntarily for a man other than the opposing queen. It will be seen from diagram 1 that the queen, if centrally placed, controls almost half of an unrestricted board.

The Rook (♜♜)

The rook, sometimes referred to as the castle, may move in a *vertical* or *horizontal* direction only, over any number of squares that may be vacant. It captures in the same manner as the queen, occupying the square on which the hostile man stands, whilst removing it from the board. Note that wherever a rook stands on an empty board, it commands fourteen squares.

The Bishop (♝♝)

The bishop moves *diagonally* only, over any number of squares that may be vacant, capturing in the same manner as the preceding pieces. Note that a bishop is restricted to the squares of one colour only, and that the nearer it stands to the edge of the board, the fewer the squares it controls.

DIAGRAM 2

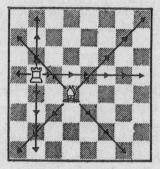

THE ROOK AND BISHOP

From the foregoing it will be clear that the queen combines the moves of rook and bishop. If the queen is moved vertically or horizontally over an odd number of squares, she will then command diagonals of the opposite colour, a property with which the bishop is not endowed.

The Knight (♘ ♞)

The move of the knight occasions some beginners difficulty, although there is no reason why this should be so. The move is best defined as from one corner of a 3 × 2 rectangle to the opposite corner. Diagram 3 should make this clear. In the case of the knight, as in the case of the king, no extension of the move (endorsed by the phrase " over any number of squares that may be vacant ") is permitted.

Men standing on intervening squares do not affect the knight's move. For this reason, some players are inclined to talk of a knight " jumping " or " moving between " other men. These terms are strictly incorrect; the movement of the piece from one square to another is completely detached from external considerations.

DIAGRAM 3

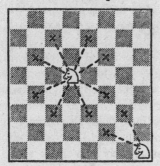

THE KNIGHT

The knight captures in occupying, as is the case with the other pieces. It is strongest on a crowded board, when it can pursue its designs unimpeded, and is very much weaker on an open board when the mobility of the other pieces is proportionately increased.

It will be noted, also, that the knight, like the king, queen and bishop, controls fewer squares when stationed on or near the edge of the board. Also, that if on a white square it controls only black squares and vice-versa.

To the beginner, who overestimates their powers,

knights are sinister creatures, to be jealously guarded if friendly and ruthlessly hunted if hostile. Their fascination is undoubtedly due to their peculiar move—a shifty side-step that arouses instant suspicion in a player unversed in their limitations.

The Pawn (♙ ♟)

The pawn, unlike the pieces, moves in a forward direction only, one square at a time.

Each pawn has, however, the option of moving two squares forward on its first move, and this right is retained throughout the game, always provided the pawn has not been moved.

The pawn, alone of all the chessmen, captures in a different manner to which it moves. Whereas it *moves* one square straight forward, it *captures* one square diagonally forward. A pawn may not move diagonally forward unless, in so doing, it captures an opposing man; nor may it move straight forward, either one or two squares, unless such squares are vacant.

The initial double move of the pawn was introduced to stimulate what would otherwise be a slow game. However, in order that a pawn should not take advantage of the double move to evade a hostile pawn, a rule, known as the " *en passant* " (Fr.: " in passing ") rule was introduced.

This lays down that if a pawn, moving two squares forward from its initial position, could have been captured by an opposing pawn *if it had only moved one square*, then such capture may be effected as if the pawn had only moved one square. That is to say, the pawn making the initial double move is removed from the board, the capturing pawn occupying the square that the captured pawn would have occupied had it only moved one. The right to make a capture " *en passant* " is forfeited if not exercised the move immediately subsequent. Note that a pawn can only be captured " *en passant* " by another pawn, and not by a piece.

A pawn on reaching the end of the board (the last rank of eight squares) is promoted to any piece (other than a king) that the player chooses. A queen is the natural selection, in view of her being the strongest piece, but occasionally the peculiarity of the position demands promotion to knight, or even to bishop or rook.

DIAGRAM 4

(a) BLACK (b)

(c) WHITE (d)

THE PAWN

A parallel to pawn-promotion may be drawn with the army, where a soldier, after long and meritorious service, is promoted to officer rank.

No restriction is placed on the number of pawn-promotions, and although eight such promotions are perfectly possible, it is very rare that more than one or two occur in a game.

Examine the diagram (4). In this, as in all other diagrams in this book (and, indeed, in all chess literature) White is assumed to be playing UP the board, Black DOWN the board. For purposes of economy, four separate positions are given on the one diagram, but in each case the whole of the board is assumed to be included.

In (a) none of the four pawns can move. In (b) the white pawn can capture either the rook or the bishop, or it can move straight ahead on to the white square. In each of these cases it has reached the eighth rank, or end of the board, and must be simultaneously promoted to a piece which is placed on the square to which the pawn moves. If a queen is desired, and the white queen is still on the board, a reversed rook or a coin will symbolise the promotion, and serve the purpose.

In (c) the white pawns stand in their initial positions, as will be clear from diagram 5. Hence the two outside pawns can both be advanced one or two squares. Both can also capture the black pawn. The black pawn can capture either of these two pawns, whilst the middle white pawn is unable to move.

In (d) the white pawn has just made the initial double move, and Black can consequently capture " *en passant* " as shown.

Pawns are usually viewed with disfavour by the tyro, who considers they hinder the movement of the pieces. He is apt to surrender them cheerfully, at the least provocation, in blissful ignorance that his recurrent defeats are in any way linked with their loss. This, as he soon learns, is a grave mistake, for the strength of the game is based largely on the pawn play.

An Aide Memoir

To assist the memory, here is a short verse outlining the moves of the various men :

> The KING may move a single square in any free direction;
>
> Should he succumb the game is lost, so play with circumspection!
>
> To crossword clues the ROOK may take—it moves across and down;
>
> If lines are clear it changes gear and really goes to town.
>
> The BISHOP travels cornerwise if ways are unrestricted,
>
> His diocese but half the board—the rest is interdicted.
>
> The QUEEN may radiate at will if she is not obstructed;
>
> Like rook or bishop, as required, her journeys are conducted.
>
> The KNIGHT, a problem child, extends (according to decree)
>
> To the diametric corner of a figure two by three.
>
> The PAWN moves only forward, and but a single square;
>
> Is promoted on the eighth rank (assume it reaches there).
>
> Initially, however, its functions to enhance,
>
> The pawn retains the option of a double-square advance.

.   .   .   .   .

Initial Position

Having seen how the chessmen move, let us now set

them up in their initial positions, preparatory to the commencement of a game (Diagram 5).

Note that the board is orientated so that there is a black square in the left-hand corner. It is surprising how often even experienced players forget this, until their sense that "something is wrong" leads them to discover the error.

DIAGRAM 5

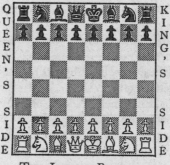

THE INITIAL POSITION

In the four corners of the board are the rooks, next to them the knights, then the bishops and finally the royal couples—the queens on the squares of their own colour (black queen on black square, white queen on white square).

The pawns are then arrayed in front of their respective pieces. Notice carefully the asymmetrical arrangement of the kings and queens—each piece opposite its rival counterpart.

In chess, White always moves first (choice of colour is decided by sortilege: it is common for one player to conceal two pawns, one white and one black, in his clenched fists, the opponent then choosing " which hand " to determine forces).

Before we can start playing an actual game, however, there are one or two more important rules to be learned; after which it will be necessary to become familiar with a few rudimentary manoeuvres. Chess, to be learnt properly, must be studied step by step, each point being thoroughly assimilated before passing on to the next one, too rapid advancement leading only to confusion and eventual frustration.

Castling

Castling is a privilege to which both sides are entitled once in a game. The manoeuvre, which is a joint move of king and one rook, counts as a single move. It may be played only if all the following conditions are fulfilled:

(1) Neither the king nor the rook have moved.

(2) The king is not in check.

(3) There are no pieces, either hostile or friendly, between the king and the rook, nor does an enemy man attack a square over which, or on to which the king must move.

There is a common idea in circulation that one may not castle once the king has been in check. This is incorrect: provided that, in getting out of check the king was not moved (thereby contravening (1) above), castling is permitted.

In castling, the king is moved two squares in the direction of the rook, which is brought over next to the king on the inside. The move is then complete.

Castling may take place on either side of the board, and is referred to as K-side castling and Q-side castling. Once castling is complete the pieces reassume their normal functions and the manoeuvre can on no account be retracted.

The object of the move is two-fold: it brings a rook into play in the centre of the board and gives greater security to the king. It is normally utilised by both players during the course of a game.

DIAGRAM 6

BLACK

WHITE

CASTLING

Examine diagram 6. White may castle on *either* side (the movements of the pieces are indicated by arrows), whereas Black may not castle at all, since the rook on the Q-side has been moved, and to castle K-side the black king would have to pass over a square commanded by an enemy piece (the white bishop).

Checkmate

We have seen that if a king is attacked (in check) and cannot be moved out of check, nor can the attacking unit be removed or a friendly man interposed, the king is assumed to be captured (checkmated) and the game is over.

Here are four examples in each of which the black king is mated. In diagram 7 (a) the black king is attacked by the white queen, which also controls all the neighbouring squares. Since the white queen is protected by the white king she may not be captured, and Black has consequently lost the game. In (b) the black king is attacked by the white pawn, which is defended by the second white pawn. The knight controls the two remaining squares in the vicinity of the king (" the king's field "), who is therefore checkmated.

DIAGRAM 7

(a)   BLACK   (b)

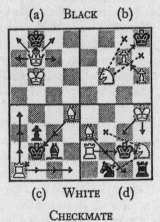

(c)   WHITE   (d)

CHECKMATE

In (c) the black king is again attacked, this time by the white bishop, which also indirectly guards the rook, as if the black king captured the rook he would still be in check, and, as we have seen, this would constitute an illegal move.

The white rook controls no less than four of the squares in the king's field, the only two remaining escape squares being occupied by black men. The pawn is unable to move (remember, White is playing UP the board, Black is playing DOWN), and the black bishop, only capable of moving on white squares, is unable to intervene. Both the black men are restricting the movement of the black king, and are said to be creating " self-blocks ".

In (d) the position is more complex and should be examined carefully. The black king is attacked by the white rook, which is also indirectly defending the knight. The white king controls two escape squares, the bishop one and the knight one. Neither the black rook nor the black knight can capture the attacking piece, nor can either interpose between it and the black king. Black is checkmated. Note that if the black rook and knight were interchanged, either of them would be able to move onto the black square between the black king and the hostile rook. If, in the position given, the black knight was not on the board, the black king would still be checkmated, since the white knight attacks the vacated square.

If the black rook was off the board, however, the black king would be able to move out of check into the corner. All the white pieces are clearly indispensable to the mate in the position given.

Stalemate

Occasionally a position arises (usually when there are only a few pieces left on the board) when one side, whose turn it is to move, is unable to do so. If the king were in check, the position would be checkmate, as above. If, however, the king is not in check, the position is known as stalemate, and the game is adjudged a draw.

This term has been adopted by military and political writers to describe a position in which the status quo is likely to be maintained, and the metaphor, although not strictly apposite, is a good one.

In diagram 8 (a) the white queen controls the three squares in the king's field, *but she is not attacking the king*. If Black has no other pieces on the board, the position would be stalemate with Black to move.   In (b), similarly, the bishops control the king's escape squares.   The pawn is unable to move, and, since the king is not in check, and it is Black's turn to play, White is said to have stalemated Black and the game is a draw.

DIAGRAM 8

(a)   BLACK   (b)

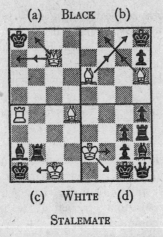

(c)   WHITE   (d)

STALEMATE

In (c), the black king's only square is next to the white king—to occupy which would constitute an illegal move. A move by the black bishop would expose the king to an attack from the white rook—again illegal. The black rook is in the same dilemma; any move exposing the king to check from the white bishop. These two black pieces are said to be " pinned ". As neither can move, with Black's turn to play the game is drawn. If it were White's turn to play, however, the bishop could capture the rook delivering checkmate.

In (d) it will be seen that none of the black men can move—the pawns obstructing the pieces. Black, to play, is stalemated. The possibility of such a position as this occurring in an actual game is remote.

Stalemates are not common in chess, although the threat of stalemate (or rather deliberate self-stalemate) by the player with the weaker force is often encountered.

Other Methods of Concluding a Game

Apart from checkmate and stalemate, there are several other ways by which a game may be concluded.

(1) INSUFFICIENT FORCE

If neither side has sufficient force left to checkmate the opposing king, the game is drawn. What constitutes insufficient force will be seen in the next chapter.

(2) PERPETUAL CHECK

If one side is able to submit the enemy king to a perpetual series of checks, the game is drawn. Clearly it will not be to the advantage of the stronger side to resort to a " perpetual " (as perpetual check is more commonly called).

(3) REPETITION OF MOVES

If the same position occurs three times in a game, with the same player to move in each case, either side may claim a draw.

(4) FIFTY MOVE RULE

If each side plays fifty consecutive moves without making a single capture or pawn move, either player may claim a draw. This rule, which was created to prevent a game continuing ad infinitum, is very rarely applied.

(5) DRAW BY MUTUAL AGREEMENT

The players may at any time agree to a draw. Positions are often reached where neither player can lay claim to a winning advantage, and both players are reluctant to embark on doubtful ventures that would be more than likely to recoil on the initiator. In such positions, a draw is commonly agreed. A very high percentage of master games finish in this fashion.

(6) RESIGNATION

A player who sees the position is hopeless, and that disaster is inevitable sooner or later, will " resign " (concede) the game. More than half of all chess games conclude in this manner. The beginner, however, will very rarely resign, either because he is not aware of the dangers that threaten or because he is hopeful of his opponent blundering.

In point of fact, it is inadvisable for the tyro to surrender in this manner, as he will learn much more of the game from being checkmated a few dozen times. Later, however, resignation in irredeemable positions is desirable, since much time is thus saved. A few novices consider that holding out to the bitter end constitutes courage. On the contrary, chess etiquette requires that a player who is clearly beaten shall resign in good grace. A player who continues the struggle can only be prolonging the game in the hope that his opponent will make a mistake—a discourteous imputation of an adversary's ability, and the height of bad chess manners. But, to repeat, every game should be played to a finish in the initial stages of instruction.

In addition to those given above, there are some other ways in which the result of a game may be determined. These, however, have only to do with such matters as the players' conduct and necessary legal niceties associated with match and tournament games, and they need not concern us here.

Chess Notation

It is one of the merits of chess that moves can be easily recorded. This has made possible an impressive literature of the game, and the accumulation of a vast number of master games played during the last hundred years or so. In the leisure and comfort of your home you can recreate world championship encounters or, if you so wish, play through the records of your own games in order to discover your errors and improve your play.

There are two common notations in use, the Descriptive (or English) and the Algebraic. The Descriptive is the most widely used in the English-speaking world and so has been adopted for this book. The Algebraic, together with the Forsyth notation (used for recording positions) are explained in Chapter IX.

The Descriptive (or English) Notation

The chess board is nominally divided into two sides, the king's side and the queen's side. In the initial position (diagram 5, page 20) it will be seen that that half of the board in which the two kings stand is known as the king's side; the other half, in which the queens stand, the queen's side. Each rook, bishop and knight is designated according to which side of the board it is placed in the initial position. Thus in diagram 5, the white pieces, reading from left to right, are queen's rook, queen's knight, queen's bishop, queen, king, king's bishop, king's knight, king's rook.

The chessboard is further considered to consist of eight files (vertical) and eight ranks (horizontal). The files are referred to by relation to the pieces in the initial position. Again in diagram 5, we read from left to right: queen's rook's file, queen's knight's file, queen's bishop's file, queen's file, etc. Note that this applies equally to White and Black.

Pawns are always described by the files on which they stand; one speaks of the queen's pawn, the king's rook's pawn and so on. The pieces, unlike the pawns, retain their initial classification throughout the game regardless of their position on the board.

The ranks are numbered one to eight, each player referring to his back rank as the first, the next (on which the pawns stand) the second, and so forth. Here it will be noted that White's third rank, for example, is Black's sixth; Black's second rank White's seventh, etc.

The board and men have now been classified; there remain the squares. These are named after the rank and file on which they are situated. The square on which the queen's rook stands in the initial position is called queen's rook's one (or queen's rook's square) or simply QR1. The queen's rook's pawn (QRP) stands on QR2, the opposing QPR on QR7, the opposing QR on QR8. Other abbreviations employed in respect of the chessmen are: K (king), B (bishop), Kt (knight). The knight is occasionally abbreviated to N or S (Ger.: Springer) to differentiate it from the king.

Examine diagram 9. Here the files are indicated, and the ranks numbered. Write down the squares on which each of the chessmen stands. Thus; WK (white king) on KB2 (king's bishop's second). WBs (white bishops) on KB1 and Q6 (king's bishop's one and queen's six). Remember that the black men are reckoned from Black's side of the board; the solitary black pawn is on Q7, not Q2.

Chess Moves

The board, men and squares having been duly labelled for identification, we can now turn our attention to the ultimate function of notation—the recording of actual moves.

DIAGRAM 9

CHESS NOTATION

Suppose, in the diagram, it is Black's turn to play

and he wishes to move his king onto the queen's square immediately to his right. Then the move is written K (king—the man being moved) - (hyphen, implying " to ") Q1 (queen's square, or queen one), K-Q1.

If it were White's turn to play, and he wished to make the initial two-square jump with his king's knight's pawn, the move could be described as KKtP-KKt4. But nine symbols for one simple move is long-winded and unnecessary. It is clear from the position that no white pawn can move to QKt4, since that square is occupied by a rook; hence the reference " Kt4 " is sufficient. Also, as we recall that all pawns move in a forward direction only, it is evident that no other pawn except the KKtP can move to (K)Kt4. Therefore we can write simply P-Kt4. The rule to remember is that the qualifying " king's " or " queen's ", either applied to the man or to the square, is unnecessary if ambiguity is not created.

If White wants to play KRP-KR4 however, we note that P-R4 will not do, as the QRP can also move to (Q)R4. Therefore we must qualify the square: P-KR4 is correct. Neither the QRP nor any other but the KRP can move to KR4, so that further qualification (of the man) can be dispensed with.

Another case of ambiguity would arise if White desired to move the bishop on KB1 to QB4. B-B4 would not do, as that might be taken to infer a movement of the bishop on Q6 to KB4. Here again square qualification is necessary: B-QB4 is correct (it is clear the other white bishop cannot move to QB4).

When one man captures another, the hyphen, indicating " to " is replaced by a cross (×), meaning " captures " or " takes ". If White wants to capture the pawn standing on QB5 (Black would call this square

QB4, remember) with his bishop on Q6, the move would be expressed as B × P. No question of confusion arises, as neither of the white bishops can capture any other black pawn in the position.

If, however, White wished to take the black knight on QKt3 (Black's QKt6) with his rook on Kt4, R × Kt would not be sufficient, since it would not be clear, on paper, which of the rooks was effecting the capture. If the rook on Kt4 was the queen's rook, the move could be recorded correctly as QR × Kt, but during the course of the game it is very possible that White has forgotten which rook is which (a few chess sets have small crowns stamped on the king's side pieces to facilitate reference, but such sets are uncommon). He must therefore resort to some other means of differentiating between the two pieces. This is done by referring, in brackets, to the square on which the piece effecting the capture stands, viz: R(Kt4) × Kt; or, sometimes, R(4) × Kt.

If White desired instead to capture this knight with the pawn on QR2, P × Kt would again be not sufficient, as this might also be read as P(Q5) × Kt(K6). Where there is the choice of two pieces to be captured, the square is usually designated by the captured unit thus: P × Kt (Kt3) or P × Kt (3), although RP × Kt or P × K (or Q)Kt would be equally correct.

If, in the diagrammed position (9), Black had just played the QBP from B2 to B4, the white pawn on Q5 could capture " *en passant* ". This would be recorded as P × P e.p. It will be seen that Black (assuming he has not moved his king or QR) can castle on the queen's side, but not on the king's side (because the white bishop controls his KB1 over which the king must pass). This move would be scored as O-O-O, castling on the king's side as O-O (some chess books do not trouble with notation here, referring simply to "Castles QR" or "Castles KR"). To remember the distinction between the two, the QR moves three squares in castling queen's side (O-O-O), the KR two squares in castling king's side (O-O).

Returning to diagram 9, supposing Black decided instead to promote the pawn on Q7, by playing it one square forward to the eighth (White's first) rank. This move would be recorded as P-Q8(=Q), or P-Q8(Q), assuming that the promotion was to a queen. Suppose Black wished to promote the pawn to a knight, however. The presence of both his original knights on the board in no way prohibits this, a belief held by some beginners (in the medieval game such a rule did exist, and, indeed, obtains in some remote areas of the world to-day). So Black plays P-Q8(Kt). But wait! The white king is in check from the knight. This is shown by the symbol (+) or by the abbreviation (ch). Hence the completed move would read P-Q8(Kt) ch.

Similarly if White had played B-Kt5 (only one bishop, that on KB1, can go to Kt5), the piece would be attacking the black king, and the abbreviation would have to be added: B-Kt5 ch.

Checkmate is simply written "mate", and a double check (when a king is attacked by two enemy units simultaneously—a manoeuvre which will be explained in the next chapter) as dbl. ch. A discovered check (the piece moving disclosing a check from a piece behind) is similarly abbreviated to dis. ch.

Finally, exclamation and question marks may be used in annotations to denote good and bad moves respectively.

B

Conclusion

If the reader has studied this chapter at a single sitting, he will probably be in a state of near mental exhaustion. He has possibly already forgotten how the knight moves, or what stalemate is; but he should not let this worry him.

He has the consolation of knowing that there are only a few very minor rules still to be learned, the rest of the book being devoted to the right way to play the game.

The chapter should be re-read carefully after a short interval, and before going on, the reader should be thoroughly conversant with the moves of the pieces, pawn promotion, check and checkmate, stalemate, castling and chess notation. A good idea is to place half-a-dozen pieces haphazardly on the board and move them around, black and white alternately, capturing, checking, and, if possible, securing positions in which checkmate or stalemate may be given. Then try recording moves, remembering that they are reckoned from the side of the player in each case (the board can be turned round each time to make it easier).

By way of a test, return to diagram 9 and see how many of the following questions you can answer correctly: (answers on page 35):

(1) How many men in the position given are unable to move?

(2) To how many squares can the white bishop on Q6 move?

(3) How many men are on their original squares?

(4) Can White play K-K1?

(5) If Black, to move, captures the pawn on Kt3 with his QRP, how should this move be recorded?

(6) On the whole board how many possible (i.e., legal) black moves are there (count the pawn promotion as one move)?

Solutions to Test (Chapter One)

(1) One. Black's QKtP.
(2) Eight, including the pawn capture.
(3) Ten: White B on KB1, Ps on KR2, KKt2, QR2.
       Black K on K1, Rs on KR1 and QR1, Ps on KR2, QKt2, QR2.
(4) No; because he would then be in check from the black pawn.
(5) P × P.
(6) Twenty-nine.

CHAPTER II

RUDIMENTARY THEORY

Relative Values of the Chessmen

The reader will no doubt have gathered by this time that the chessmen, being possessed of intrinsic qualities of movement and capture, may also be compared, one with the other, on the yardstick of relative values.

The correlation of the powers of the pieces is deceptive, however, as in any position each man will be possessed of a power peculiar to that position. In diagram 9, page 30, for example, both black rooks are out of play, whereas the humble pawn on Q7, threatening, if unwatched, to become a queen, is an apparent force. However, the pawn may soon fall, and the black rooks may bring their long-range guns to bear down the vital files. A game is therefore in a permanent state of flux, and force values change from move to move. The scale of relative values can only remain a guide governing the exchange of pieces (an exchange is when one side captures an opposing man, giving up one of his own men in the process) when other considerations are approximately equal. The ability to assess the true value of a position and, in consequence, the extempore values of the men composing the position, is a gift with which only really strong chess-players are endowed.

The king, since he cannot be captured, and is only used as an attacking piece towards the end of the game when his powers are approximately equal to those of a bishop, is excluded from the assessment.

Queen = two Rooks
Bishop = Knight
Rook = Bishop and two Pawns
Bishop (or Knight) = three Pawns

These are approximations. The bishop is normally worth a fraction more than the knight, two bishops being substantially stronger than two knights.

It is advisable for the novice, in his earlier games, to base his judgments on the above scale.

Rudimentary Positions
(a) The Pin

As we have seen in position (c), diagram 8, page 25,

DIAGRAM 10

(a)   BLACK   (b)

(c)   WHITE   (d)

RUDIMENTARY MANOEUVRES

a piece is pinned if, in moving, it would expose the king to a hostile check. In diagram 10 (a), the knight is also said to be pinned, for although it may be legally moved, the white bishop would then capture the black queen which, as can be seen from the table of relative values, would be a poor bargain for Black even should the bishop then fall.

The term " pin " is thus extended to signify any position in which the movement of a man would expose another man to attack from a weaker piece. If there was another black knight at QB2 (that is, on the diagonal between the queen and the other knight), the set-up would be known as a half-pin as the movement of either knight would automatically result in the pinning of the other.

(b) Double Check

In the second example (diagram 10(b)) we see a double check, when a king is exposed to attack from two hostile men simultaneously. White has just moved the rook, as indicated. In a double check the king must move, since he cannot capture both attacking men or interpose two of his own men in one move. If he cannot move, as in the diagram, he is checkmated. Note that Black can apparently capture either piece with the rook, or interpose the queen between either the king and rook or the king and bishop, but none of these resources are open to him because whichever he adopts the king will still be in check from the remaining white piece.

The extraordinary power of the double check is apparent, and it is something a player should endeavour to avoid unless he is certain that such check would be innocuous—which is very rarely the case.

(c) Discovered Check

This is similar to the double check, but not as dangerous,

as the piece moved does not itself give check. If in diagram 10(b), the white rook had moved to B7 instead of B8 it would then have been a " discovered " and not a " double " check. Black could thus have avoided mate, but would have lost the queen.

(d) Through Check

The position in 10 (c) is something to guard against. Here the black king, in check, is compelled to move, when the bishop will capture the black queen.

(e) The Fork

The knight, by virtue of its irregular move, can create an embarrassing attack known as a " fork ". In the position 10 (d), the knight is attacking both king and queen, and as the king must move out of check, the queen is doomed. The most common fork of the knight is of king and rook, when the rook, which, as we have seen, is the stronger piece, is lost. Forks by other pieces are possible. In diagram 4 (b) for example, the white pawn has forked the black rook and bishop. The term is self-explanatory.

Endings

In order to acquaint the reader with the practical power of the pieces, we will examine one or two game endings.

Assuming that Black has only a king left, White will be able to force mate with a minimum force of:

(1) King and queen. White will, of course, always have his king on the board. If he has a pawn which he can safely promote, then it can be reckoned as a queen.

(2) King and rook.

(3) King and two bishops.

(4) King, bishop and knight.

Mate cannot be forced, for mathematical reasons, with:

(1) King alone—this is obvious.

(2) King and bishop.

(3) King and knight or king and two knights.

(4) Certain positions involving pawns.

It is interesting to observe that two knights (the joy of the novice!) are unable to force mate, whereas a mere pawn which can be promoted is sufficient for the purpose.

King and Queen v. King

Let us examine the system of forcing mate by king and queen against a bare king.

This performance should not demand more than ten moves, in most positions considerably fewer (when one talks of moves in chess one means moves of both sides).

Place the white king on K1, the white queen on K8, and the black king on KKt4 (White's KKt5). White can mate in a number of ways, but the principle remains the same in every case—the lone king must be driven to the edge of the board where the queen will deliver the mate, the white king assisting.

A series of checks with the queen will achieve nothing (all beginners assume that checks are stronger than quiet moves (i.e., moves that are not checks), in the hope, presumably, that " it might be mate "). White therefor moves Q-B7!, restricting the movements of the doomed monarch.

White	Black
1. Q-B7	K-Kt5

Not K-R5?, Q-Kt6! further restricting the king.

| 2. K-B2 | K-Kt4 |
| 3. K-Kt3 | K-R3 |

The only square.

4. Q-Kt8

K-B4? would be a grave error, since the black king would then be without a move—stalemated, in other words.

| 4 | K-R4 |

Again the only move.

| 5. K-B4 | K-R3 |

Not K-R5? allowing White to mate immediately.

6. K-B5

And now mate next move is unavoidable.

| 6. | K-R4 |

7. Q-Kt5 mate.

The black king has been forced to the edge of the board and is there checkmated. King and queen cannot mate a bare king anywhere except at the side: the same applies to king and rook against bare king, as the following example shows.

King and Rook v. King

Set up the kings as before, and substitute a white rook for the queen. Since this mate is more difficult, as might be expected, and as it is one which you are likely to encounter (if your opponent obstinately refuses to resign), it is essential to be familiar with the correct procedure.

White	Black
1. R-KB8	

Again limiting the black king.

1.		K-Kt5
2.	K-K2	K-Kt6
3.	K-K3	K-Kt5
4.	R-B1	K-Kt4

Both sides are playing the best moves.

5.	K-K4	K-Kt3
6.	K-K5	K-Kt2
7.	K-K6	K-Kt3
8.	R-KKt1 ch.	

The king is now forced to the edge of the board. Note the position of the white king at the precise moment of the check: it is directly opposite the black king, thereby controlling all the three squares which might otherwise have been open to the fugitive. The black king is now confined to the rook's file, and White endeavours to set up the same position in order to deliver the coup-de-grace.

8.		K-R4
9.	K-B5	K-R5
10.	R-Kt8	K-R6
11.	K-B4	K-R7
12.	K-B3	K-R8
13.	K-B2	K-R7

The black king is now forced to come back opposite the white king: the curtain falls.

14. R-R8 mate.

The maximum number of moves required for this type of ending is seventeen—and this only in extreme cases.

King and two Rooks v. King

This is a very easy ending, the two rooks being moved

rank by rank or file by file, to the edge of the board where the lone king is checkmated. Place the white king on K1, the two white rooks on QR1 and KR1, and the black king on K5. White mates in eight moves by: 1. QR-R3 (KR-R3 also forces mate in eight), K-B5. 2. KR-R4 ch., K-Kt4. 3. R-Kt4 (as no check is announced this must be QKt4), K-B4. 4. R-R5 ch., K-K3. 5. R-Kt6 ch., K-Q2. 6. R-R7 ch., K-B1. 7. R-R7, K-Q1. 8. R-Kt 8 mate.

King and two Bishops v. King

The ending with king and two bishops embraces the same idea of driving the lone king to the edge of the board, the pieces working in conjunction to cut-off the escape squares (or flight squares, as they are more commonly called). The king must be mated on a corner square, and in this respect the mate differs from the endings with queen and rook given above.

King, Bishop and Knight v. King

The ending with king, bishop and knight against bare king is conducted in the same manner as the ending with the two bishops, except that the victim must be mated on a corner square of the same colour as that on which the bishop stands.

Most elementary text-books on chess give pages of analysis on these two endings which serve only to bewilder the student. Many experienced players are unable to force the mate with bishop and knight. And, indeed, why worry? In my experience I have never played or seen played an ending of this nature. Archaic instruction is almost always a forerunner of boredom and disinterest.

King and Pawn Endings

When the tumult of the middle-game has subsided into the comparative quiet of the end-game, it is usual for each side to be left with a few pawns and perhaps a piece or two. With only a handful of men remaining it is easier to calculate with precision the best line of play—indeed, the end-game of chess is a fine art, and there are many books devoted to this subject alone.

With only limited force available, it is unlikely that either king is in danger of being mated. The play is therefore concentrated on the task of queening (promoting) pawns—which does not mean to say that either player should lose sight of mating possibilities.

As soon as one side succeeds in promoting a pawn, he will obviously have a decided, if not decisive advantage, and can then turn his attention to destroying the enemy force preparatory to the final check-mate.

On a crowded board the likelihood of a pawn surviving the hazardous march from the second to the eighth rank is remote; but as the forces decrease its power augments. It will be seen, therefore, that in the end-game the pawn takes on a new importance, since the longer it survives the greater are its chances of eventual promotion.

To understand even the simplest end-games, it is necessary to study the movements of the pawn in conjunction with the movements of the friendly king vis-à-vis the hostile king.

Look at the diagram (11). Here are four simple examples of king and pawn endings.

In (a), Black to move is a draw, since the king is stalemated. White, to move, wins, however. 1. K-B6, K-R2 (the only move). 2. K-B7 (still guarding the pawn and preventing Black returning to the promotion square),

K-R3 (again the only move). 3. P-Kt8(Q) and White mates in two. 3. .... K-R4. 4. Q-Kt3, K-R3. 5. Q-Kt6 mate.

In (b), Black to move is a draw (stalemate). If White to move, he is in a quandary. The only square to which he can play the king and still guard the pawn (Kt6) leaves the black king in stalemate, whilst any other king move permits Black to capture the pawn. From which we derive the important precept that if, in a king and rook's pawn v. king ending, the solitary king can reach the queening square before the pawn, the game is drawn.

(a)   DIAGRAM 11   (b)

(c)   PAWN-PLAY   (d)

The difference between 11 (a) and 11 (b) will now be apparent. In (a) the white king penetrates by forcing the black king out on the opposite file; whereas in (b) he is not able to do this.

In (c) the king is unable to capture either pawn without permitting the other to queen. For example: 1. K-B3, P-R6. 2. K × P, P-R7 and queens next move. White can only shuffle his king impotently until the black king arrives on the scene to force the issue. Black loses both pawns if he attempts to promote them without assistance: 1. K-Kt1!, P-B6?. 2. K-B2, P-R6. 3. K × P, P-R7. 4. K-Kt2.

In (d) White can again do nothing but move his king around until the black king arrives. If he capture the unprotected pawn he cannot stop the other one queening.

Promotion Square

A simple rule for determining whether a pawn, advancing alone to promotion, can be captured by the king before it reaches the queening square, is illustrated in diagram 12.

DIAGRAM 12

BLACK

WHITE

THE QUEENING SQUARE

Imagine a square with one side embracing the path from pawn to queening square. If the black king can move inside this square he can capture the pawn. In the diagram, Black, with the move, draws by playing K-B6 or K-B5. White, with the move, wins by P-R4, and the pawn cannot be stopped. If the pawn were at R2, White would still win by virtue of the initial double pawn move 1. P-R4. This rule only applies to a pawn advancing alone: if the White king or other man can in any way influence the play, the formula does not apply.

Conclusion

The reader should now be possessed of a reasonable grasp of the elementary principles of the game. In order that he may not become over-wearied with theory we shall proceed to play over a short game or two, assessing the value of each move as we go.

Before passing on, however, try the following brief test based on the points we have examined:

(Answers on page 48).

(1) Place WK on QR8, WKt on K3; BK on KR3, BQ on KR7, BB on QKt1. Black here plays B-R2, attacking the knight and threatening Q-Kt1 mate. What result?

(2) In the king and queen ending given in this chapter, after Black played 6. . . . K-R4, White mated by 7. Q-Kt5. Can you see any alternative mates for White in this position (one move only!)?

(3) Place WK on QR1, WP on QR4; BK on KB4. Can Black, to move, prevent the white pawn queening?

(4) Place WK on Q6, R on Q1; BK on K1. White to play. Mate in how many moves?

(5) Place WK on KR5, P on KB7; BK on KR2. White to play.   What result?

(6) Place WK on QKt5, P on QKt6; BK on QKt1. (i) White to move—what result? (ii) Black to move—what result?

Solutions to Test (Chapter Two)

(1) Draw.   White can play Kt-Kt4 ch! forking king and queen, thus leaving both sides with insufficient mating force. If White plays K × B?, Black plays simply Q-KB7 pinning the knight, capturing it next move and winning easily with king and queen against king.

(2) Q-KR8 or Q-R7—here the queen, it will be noticed, is only exercising her powers as a rook.

(3) Yes, by K-K3, K-K4 or K-K5.

(4) Two: 1. R-KB1!, K-Q1.   2. R-B8 mate.

(5) White wins: 1. P-B8(R)!, etc. Not P-B8(Q) stalemate, or P-B8(B) or (Kt) with insufficient mating force. Black to play draws by K-Kt2 followed by K × P.

(6) Draw in each case. (i) 1. K-R6, K-R1 (not K-B1?, K-R7). 2. P-Kt7 ch., K-Kt1; and White must now give up the pawn or stalemate the black king.

(ii) 1. ... K-Kt2! and White can do nothing except move his king about on the fifth rank, for Black plays forwards and backwards from Kt1 to Kt2. If the white king tries to penetrate the sequel is as in (i).   Note that 1.... K-R1 (or 1 ... K-B1) would be instantly fatal: 2. K-R6 (or B6), K-Kt1. 3. P-Kt7 and wins (see diagram 11 (a), page 45). On examination it will be seen that if one side can play a pawn to the seventh rank in this type of ending *without giving check,* and provided that the pawn is not a rook's pawn, he will win.

CHAPTER III

EXAMPLES OF PLAY

The object of the game, we know, is to checkmate the opposing king. Since a direct assault is not always possible (and might result in placing one's own king in jeopardy) other, more immediate targets, must be found.

Three factors dominate the play:

(i) Time—represented by the moves of the men.

(ii) Force—represented by the powers of the men.

(iii) Space—represented by the territory controlled by the men.

A gain in time (or " tempo " as it is called), by forcing your opponent to waste moves, permits you to marshal your forces effectively and swiftly.

A gain in force by, say, capturing an enemy rook for a bishop or a knight (known as " winning the exchange ") is clearly advantageous.

A gain in space—extending your territorial control, thereby achieving greater manoeuvrability for your pieces—is again an obvious advantage.

Bearing these three points in mind, in addition to the ultimate aim of mating the opposing king, every move in a game should be made to some purpose.

The player who has no plan, and who aimlessly shifts his men around as the fancy takes him, will rarely hold out for longer than a dozen or so moves. Better—far better— to have a bad plan than to have no plan at all. Which does not mean that a course of action, once formulated, should be adhered to obstinately; but rather that it should be modified or recast if necessary to meet changing conditions.

Remember, therefore, to play with a purpose at all times.

In chess, as in war, movements are governed by two determining factors—strategy and tactics. Strategy can be said to consist of the spade-work; tactics, which implements strategy, the point-to-point struggle.

Some players prefer the subtleties of finer strategy, others the exhilarating rough-and-tumble of tactical play; it is this distinction which to a greater or lesser degree determines a player's style.

So much for theory, and we are now ready to play over an actual game. The men are set up as in diagram 5, page 20 (black square left-hand corner!) and White moves first.

White	*Black*
1. P-K4	

Pawn to king four. An excellent move. Note that the king's bishop and the queen are now free (in the initial position only the pawns and the knights are able to move). This pawn advance also strikes at the centre, which is the most important area of the board and the focus of all opening play.

1.	
	P-K4

The same. One of Black's best replies. Clearly it achieves the same as White's move. Note that now neither of these pawns can move.

2. Kt-KB3

The king's knight is brought into play. It attacks the

black pawn and is therefore an aggressive move. It also attacks the square Q4.

2.   Kt-QB3.

Obvious and best. The pawn is now guarded, and the knight counter attacks White's Q4 square. It will be observed that the game to this point has revolved round the four centre squares. The struggle for these squares, control of which always yields the superior game, motivates most opening manoeuvres.

3. P-QR4

Pawn to queen's rook four. A very weak move indeed: it demonstrates White has no plan. It does not serve a single useful function, being far removed from the central locii. White has dissipated the advantage of the extra move.

3.   Kt-B3

Since the queen's knight is already at QB3, this clearly means KKt-KB3. A good move, it continues the assault on the centre, attacking White's KP.

4. Q-K2

Bad. Although this move protects the threatened pawn, it hinders the development of the king's bishop. B-Q3 in this position would have been no better, since then the queen's pawn would have been unable to move and White would have experienced difficulty in getting the queen's bishop out. Kt-B3 was correct.

4.   B-B4

Another good move which develops a piece and attacks the square Q5.

5. P-KKt3

White sees that he is unable to develop the bishop on

the long diagonal, and seeks to bring it into play via Kt2.

5.   P-Q3

Black's queen's bishop is now able to come into the game.

6. B-Kt2

The bishop is now said to be " fianchettoed " in the jargon of the chess-player. In the old-time game, before the introduction of the double pawn move, it was usual to develop the bishops in this manner, since the centre pawns, only capable of moving one square at a time, would free one bishop only to block the other. The fianchetto of the bishops has, of recent years, gained considerable popularity among the masters.

White could not, of course, play 6. B-R3 here, as the piece would then have been undefended, permitting Black to play B × B, winning a clear piece for nothing.

6.   O-O

Castles. The black king is now in comparative safety, and the rook is brought into the game.

Up to here Black's moves have been an example of model play. At some points he has had the choice of several good moves, whilst other moves could have been transposed, but his play could hardly have been improved upon.

The position in diagram 13 has now been reached. Check this with your board to ensure that the two agree. A quick assessment of the game as it stands reveals that White has decidedly the worst of it. His KB is doing nothing, his queen is no better placed at K2 than at Q1, and the QRP, a waif in the wilderness, has achieved nothing by its inconsequential advance.

Black on the other hand has his men posted to some purpose. His development (i.e., the bringing of his pieces into play) is almost complete, when he will be ready to embark on an attack. The contest may now be said to be entering the Middle-Game. There are three recognized phases in a game of chess, the Opening, Middle-Game and End-Game. There is no strict dividing line between them, the opening being understood to consist of the developing moves of each side, the middle-game

DIAGRAM 13

POSITION AFTER BLACK'S 6TH MOVE

the main struggle, the end-game when the majority of the pieces are off the board and the kings and pawns come into their own. We shall study each of these phases separately in ensuing chapters.

7. Q-Kt5

Another bad move which threatens nothing; the black bishop, knight and knight's pawn are all protected and the

KP is now unguarded. White should have again played Kt-B3.

7.   QKt-Kt5!

Since the king's knight can also go to (K)Kt5 the qualifying " QKt " is necessary.

A very strong move, hence the exclamation mark. Black now threatens to play Kt × BP ch., forking the king and the rook, with considerable material gain.

8. Kt-R3

This guards the bishop's pawn, which would now make the exchange unfavourable to Black. White could also have played K-Q1, but then the KBP would have been undefended, and, more important still, White would have forfeited the right to castle. P-B3 attacking the knight would also have been no good, since Black could still have continued Kt-B7 ch., winning the exchange at least. Q-B4 would have allowed Black to continue B-K3! attacking the queen and thereby gaining a " tempo ".

8.   B-Q2

The white queen is attacked.

9. Q-B4

Note carefully that if, in this position, White had played instead Q × P, Black would have replied R-Kt1! and the queen is without a flight square. White would then have had nothing better than to give up the queen for the rook.

9.   B-K3

Again attacking the queen.

10. Q-B3

Observe how an early foray with the queen is quickly punished. It is rarely advisable to bring the major pieces into the middle of the board at the beginning of a game, since they can be constantly harassed by the minor enemy pieces and pawns and much time is lost in the process. (The bishops and knights are known as the " minor " pieces, the rooks and queens as " major " pieces.) This move turns out to be very bad, as will be seen. Correct was Q-K2.

10.   KKt × P!

The queen is now trapped. B × P ch. would also have been playable here, but after 11. K-Q1 (not 11. K × B, KKt × P ch!, forking king and queen), Black cannot win the queen, since after KKt × P White can reply Q × Kt, the black bishop no longer defending this piece. Consequently the text move is very much stronger.

11. P-Q4

White opens the game—too late.

11.   P × P

There is no hurry to take the queen off—she is still not able to escape. Note that the king's file is now open for Black's rook.

12. Kt × P   Kt × Q

13. P × Kt

As the result of this move White has what is known as " doubled pawns "—two pawns on the same file. The QRP is now isolated, and is called an " isolated pawn ". Both these are weaknesses which we shall examine at a later stage; White's game is lost anyway.

13.   R-K1

14. P × Kt

Ignoring the " discovered check " which is threatened

by Black moving the QB, thereby exposing the white king to attack from the rook. Black has time to spare however, and first takes his piece back.

14. **B × Kt**

Attacking the QR. P-QB3 is no defence for White, as Black would play simply B × P ch., forking king and rook.

15. R-QKt1

Now Black can play to win material by B-R7 dis. ch., when White, who must first deal with the check, will lose his rook. Observe the immense power of a discovered check—the bishop can go anywhere on the board without fear of capture, because White must first attend to the attack on his king.

15. **B-B6 ch.**

Not the best. Black does not take full advantage of the position in which there are several good continuations. He is so heavily up in material however—a queen and a pawn for a knight—that it matters little.

16. K-B1

Escaping from the discovered check, but K-Q1 would have been better.

16. **B-B5 ch!**

Decisive.

17. K-Kt1

Not Kt × B?, R-K8 mate! Black sacrifices the bishop in order to clear the file for the rook. It may be argued that such an offer hardly constitutes a sacrifice. Certainly it is not a sacrifice in the true sense, but chess terminology rules that it shall be so described, so there it is.

The sacrifice is one of the keenest sources of delight to the chess-player, the apparent surrender of force creating a whimsical effect which is at once self-satisfying and artistic. This is an example of a tactical sacrifice—by far the most common. The strategical sacrifice—the relinquishing of a pawn or a piece in order to gain time or space, particularly in the opening—is more common among stronger players as it requires sound judgment.

17.   R-K8 ch.

18. B-B1
The only move.

18.   R × B ch.

Although the rook can capture *both* bishops, it can only take *one* (the KB) with check, hence the piece need not be qualified.

19. K-Kt2
The king cannot, of course, take the rook since it is defended by the QB.

19.   B-Q4 ch.

20. K-R3?
20. K × R, B × R was much better, but naturally not 20. P-B3, R × P!, when Black would again be threatening a dangerous discovered check.

20.   Q-Q2 ch.

21. K-R4
21. P-Kt4 would only have protracted the agony.

21.   B-B6.

Now mate cannot be avoided. It is often the quiet move rather than the garish check that precedes the climax.

22. K-Kt5.   Q-Kt5 checkmate.
Finis. See diagram 14.

DIAGRAM 14

FINAL POSITION

Observations

By normal standards this is a short game, the average
being around thirty-five moves. A long game will run
to sixty moves and more—sometimes into three figures.

There are a number of lessons to be learned from the
play of both sides, but the main cause of White's pre-
cipitous collapse was undoubtedly his dilatory handling
of the opening. It was evident almost from the outset
that he had no plan of campaign.

Witness Black's handling of the game by comparison—
a polished if not perfect performance.

(i) He developed his pieces quickly.

(ii) He took advantage of White's errors.

(iii) He wasted no time in side issues.

It is of particular interest to notice that Black succeeded in castling and bringing his king's rook into play, the uncastled white king offering a vulnerable target.

In the final position observe the confusion in the white ranks. The QB and KR are still "at home"; the QKt is posted at the side of the board guarding a threat which for many moves has ceased to exist; the QR has been forced to waste a tempo to avoid the attack of a minor piece; and, of course, that unhappy pawn is still forlornly standing, without rhyme or reason, on QR4. A sorry picture!

Three Brevities

The shortest game of chess possible is a brevity known as Fool's Mate. It runs to only two moves:

White	Black
1. P-KB3	P-K4
2. P-KKt4	Q-R5 mate

None of White's king's side pieces is able to interpose.

The term "Fool's Mate" is something of a misnomer, since in his early acquaintance with the game the beginner may easily overlook the vulnerability of his king, particularly when the attacking piece descends "from the blue".

On the other hand, a game concluded in four moves known as the "Scholar's Mate" is much more obvious. White wins this time:

White	Black
1. P-K4	P-K4
2. B-B4	B-B4
3. Q-R5	Kt-KB3
4. Q × BP mate	

If Black had played Kt-KB3 before he brought the bishop out all would have been well, as Q-R5 could then have been met by Kt × Q. But in any case Black had nothing to fear if he fathomed White's designs. For example, 3. . . . Q-K2, defending both the threatened mate and the KP was good since, as we have learned from the previous game, White will lose time parrying Black's imminent attacks on the wayward queen.

Variations and extensions of these two mating themes are often encountered. The KBP, against which the attack in Scholar's Mate is directed, is the weakest link in the initial position, for it is guarded only by the king. A further point in favour of castling: the rook is brought to the protection of this pawn.

Here is another short game with an attractive sacrifice:

White	Black
1. P-K4	P-K4
2. Kt-KB3	P-Q3
3. B-B4	P-KR3
4. Kt-B3	B-Kt5

Pinning the knight

5. Kt × P !
The surprise: White sacrifices the queen.

5.   B × Q
This loses, but after 5. . . . P × Kt. 6. Q × B White has won a pawn and is far ahead in development.

6. B × P ch.
That weak KBP again!

6.   K-K2

The only move; the bishop is protected by the KKt.

7. Kt-Q5 mate.

.   .   .   .   .   .

Before returning to the study of chess theory, the reader would do well to play over another game and endeavour to answer the questions posed.

Initial position again—black square left-hand corner— queens on the squares of their own colour.

White	*Black*
1. P-K4	P-K4

2. B-B4
   (a) Good or bad?

2.   Kt-QR3
   (b) Is this better than Kt-QB3?

3. Kt-KB3
   The black pawn is now attacked and is said to be " *en prise* " (Fr.: " in a position to be taken ").

3.   P-KB3?
   It is a good general rule to note that this move is almost always bad in the opening, seriously weakening the king's position.

4. Kt × P!
   A tactical sacrifice.

4.   P × Kt
   Black has nothing better.

5. Q-R5 ch.   P-KKt3
   (c) Why not 5. . . . . K-K2?

6. Q × KP ch.   Q-K2

7. Q × R   Q × P ch.

8. B-K2
    (d) Why not K-Q1 or K-B1?

8.   Kt-K2
    (e) What was White threatening?

9. P-Q3   Q × KtP

10. B-R6
    Another sacrifice.

10.   Q × R ch.

11. K-Q2   P-Q3
    (f) Why cannot Black play B × B ch.?

12. Q × B ch.   K-Q2

13. B-Kt5
    A strong move, as will be seen. The black knight
    is twice attacked, and since it cannot be further
    protected by another man, it must move or be
    captured.

13.   Kt-KB4
    (g) Why not Kt-B3?

14. Q-B7 ch.   K-B3

15. Kt-B3 !
    Another good sacrifice. The rook is "*en prise*"
    to the black queen.

15.   Q-Kt7.
    The only move. Black must keep on the diagonal
    to prevent the bishop check. If 15. . . . Q × R?
    there would follow 16. B-B3 ch., when Black
    would be mated in three at the most. How (h)?

16. R-KKt1 !

A pretty move. The QB is attacked by the black queen, so White promptly offers the rook again, hoping to decoy the queen off the vital diagonal.

16   Q × BP

Now the white KB is pinned.

17. R-KB1.

(i) If 17. B-K3, attacking the queen and guarding the rook, how would Black have continued?

17.   Q-Kt7

18. K-Q1

(j) Why?

18.   P-Q4

Clearly not 18. . . . Kt-K6 ch.?. 19. B × Kt. Or 18. . . . K-Kt3. 19. Q-Kt3 ch. Another possible line is 18. . . . Kt-Q5. 19. Q-B4 ch., Kt-B4. (19. . . . K-Q2?. 20. R-B7 ch., K-K1. 21. R-K7 ch., K-B1. 22. Q-B7 mate, or 21. . . . K-Q1. 22. Q-Kt8 mate.) 20. B-B3 ch!.—yet another sacrifice—Kt × B. 21. Q-Kt5 mate.

19. Kt × P

(k) Why not still 19. B-B3?

19.   Kt-B4

(l) Why not 19. . . . Q × Kt?

20. Q × BP ch

White, offering a further knight, wins the queen at last.

21.   K × Kt

(m) Can Black play 21. . . . K-Kt4, declining the tainted gift?

22 B-B3 ch

White misses a conclusive finish. 22. R × Kt ch.,
B (or P) × R. 23. P-B4 ch., K-Q5. (23. . . . K-K3?
24. Q-K7 mate.) 24. Q-Q6 ch., Q-Q4. 25. Q × Q
mate.

22.   Q × B ch.

23. R × Q   Resigns.

Black has two knights for a queen and a pawn.
He has no chance of redressing the balance, and his
king is in the centre of the board open to continual
attack. Under the circumstances, a graceful resignation is the best course.

Observations

This is the kind of punishment that the student must
expect to receive from the strong player. A wasted
knight move, an injudicious pawn advance and it was
virtually all over.

White sacrificed continually throughout the game
and yet won with ease. Why? Because on each
occasion he correctly assessed the relative values of the men
engaged, and played accordingly.

Sacrifices of this nature have to be very carefully
calculated, however, since a single slip in analysis would
prove disastrous to the attacker, who would find himself
unable to continue the assault with his attenuated forces.

For this reason the student is advised not to give up
voluntarily even a pawn unless he can foresee the conse-
quences. As he progresses he will often be able to sense
a sacrifice, but insight of this nature comes only with
practice.

All sacrifices should be treated on their merits alone.
Regrettably, this seemingly trite advice is rarely followed.

Beginners tend to fall into two classes; those who grab everything on the principle that they then have the superior force and it is incumbent upon the opponent to maintain the initiative; and those who never accept anything on the principle that if a man is offered it must be a trap.

If you see no objection to accepting a proffered piece, do not hesitate. An apparent sacrifice is often an oversight—the player has simply put or left a man *en prise*.

Solutions to Test—Chapter Three

(a) Good, since it develops a piece, prevents Black playing P-Q4, and attacks the weak KBP. The usual rule, and a good one to stick to when learning the game, is " knights and bishops out first ".

(b) No. It is away from the centre of the board. The knight on R3 controls four unimportant squares—exactly half the number of squares it would control on B3.

(c) Because of Q × KP checkmate!

(d) Because the bishop is " *en prise* ".

(e) 9. Q × Kt.

(f) Because the bishop is pinned by the white queen.

(g) Because of B-Kt4 mate.

(h) (1) 16. . . . P-Q4. 17. Q × QP ch., K-Kt3. 18. Q-Kt5 or Kt-R4 mate.
(2) 16. . . . K-B4. 17. Q-B4 ch. (or Q-Q5 ch.), K moves. 18. Q-Kt5 mate.
(3) 16. . . . K-Kt3. 17. Q-Kt3 ch., Kt-Kt5.

(17. . . . K-R4. 18. Q-Kt5 mate.) 18. Q × Kt ch.
K-R3. 19. Q-Kt5 mate.

(i) 17. . . . Q × QB ch!. (not 17. . . . Kt × B?.
18. Q × Q.) 18. K-Q1, Q × R ch.; and Black
wins easily, being a R, Kt and P ahead. This move
(17. B-K3) would, of course, have constituted a
first-rate blunder on White's part.

(j) To un-pin the bishop. The move threatens
19. B-B3 ch., winning the queen. Note that the
WQB is now *en prise*. White forced Black to
capture the KBP—a sacrifice that permitted the
white rook to make use of the open file to guard
the square KB3 for the projected bishop check.
If instead 18. K-B1, Black could have captured
the undefended QB with a check.

(k) Because of 18. . . . Q × R ch.

(l) Because of 20. B-B3, and the queen is pinned and
lost.

(m) No; he would then be mated by 22. P-R4 ch.,
K-R3. 23. Kt-Kt4 mate; or 22. . . . Kt × RP.
23. Q-QB4 ch., K-R4. 24. P-Kt4 mate. If
22. . . . K × P, White can mate in a number of
ways: 23. Kt-B3 ch., followed by 24. R-B4 ch.,
or 23. P-Kt3 ch., followed by 24. B-B1 ch., etc.

CHAPTER IV

POWERS OF THE CHESSMEN

If the previous chapters have been followed carefully, the reader should now have a good idea of how to play chess. Should he still be uncertain on any point he would be well advised to turn back here and dispel any doubts before proceeding further.

The last chapter was devoted to actual games, as a means of breaking the inevitable boredom that the study of page upon page of theory engenders; but now it is necessary to return to the elements of play.

As has been seen, the functions and values of the chessmen vary from stage to stage individually, collectively and relatively.

It is possible to generalise on the powers and limitations of the various men throughout the game, and to lay down broad principles for handling them.

It will be as well to repeat here that the three phases through which a game can pass are:

(a) The Opening—development of the pieces.

(b) The Middle-Game—the main struggle.

(c) The End-Game—the fight for pawn-promotion.

A game can be concluded in the opening or the middle-game without ever reaching the end-game (as in the illustrative examples in Chapter III), the three divisions having no relation to the duration of a game; that is to say, the end-game is not the last moves of any chess game, but specifically that field of play in which he

68

majority of the pieces are off the board and the kings and pawns dominate the play.

Bearing this in mind, let us examine the pieces individually under these three headings.

1. The Opening

(a) King

The king should be kept closely guarded in the opening, when a surprise attack is always a danger. Early castling is advisable, and in this respect the K-side is to be preferred to the queen's, since after the latter the QRP is unprotected.

(b) Queen

It is inadvisable to move the queen beyond the third rank where she is prone to attack from the light enemy forces. Contravention of this maxim may result in loss of time occasioned by the queen having to seek sanctuary.

(c) Rook

The rooks should be united (i.e., one guarding the other) as soon as possible. Castling is a means of achieving this aim.

Rooks should be retained on the back rank, preferably on open files.

(d) Bishop

The bishops should be developed early in the game. The best squares for posting the bishops in the opening are (1) B4, (2) Kt5 if pinning an enemy knight, (3) Kt2—the fianchetto, (4) K2 and Q2, (5) K3 and Q3 if here they do not block the advance of their respective centre pawns.

(e) Knight

Knights are employed to their best advantage in the opening. B3 is undoubtedly the most favourable post; Q2 and K2 are also not bad provided that the respective bishops are not shut in. R3 is almost always a poor square for the knight.

(f) Pawn

The first thing to remember about the pawn move—and this applies to all stages of the game—is that, unlike the pieces, it may not be retraced. In other words, a minor rubicon is crossed every time a pawn is moved; therefore all pawn moves should be made only after careful deliberation. Ask yourself: If I advance this pawn, am I likely to regret it at a later stage?

A pawn advance on one or more of the four central files is normal and necessary in the opening. A single exception may be noted: P-KB3 is almost invariably bad as it seriously weakens the king's position and takes away the best square for the KKt.

A knight's pawn may be moved a single square to permit the development of a bishop; a rook's pawn a single square to prevent the pinning of a piece on B3 by a hostile bishop on Kt4. But a good rule is: if in doubt, don't move a pawn.

2. The Middle-Game

(a) King

As in the opening, the king must be protected against attack. Towards the end of the middle-game with most of the pieces off the board, an uncastled king which is required for active service is best advanced to the second rank rather than relegated to a wing position by the no-longer useful castling.

(b) Queen

The queen is a real power, and can often be manoeuvred to attack two undefended units simultaneously, thereby winning one of them. The queen should avoid picking up stray pawns if they beguile her from the scene of activities. On the other hand, a pawn safely won is a clear advantage.

This is a further point on which the expert can be distinguished from the ordinary player—he knows which pawn can be safely captured and which pawn should be left alone.

(c) Rook

The rooks are best placed on the four centre files, particularly if any should be " open " (a file is said to be open if there are no friendly pawns on it). Doubled rooks (one behind the other) are very strong on an open file.

A rook (or better still, doubled rooks) on the seventh rank is something to be played for, as here the major pieces are immune from pawn attack, and assume the role of " cats among the pigeons ".

Rooks are especially vulnerable to attack from the bishops—particularly if the latter are working in conjunction: therefore they should, if possible, be confined to the first two ranks unless an occupation of the seventh is feasible.

(d) Bishop

The bishops are the real workers—they never relax their activities throughout the game.

They are dangerous attacking pieces, but operate best,

like the rooks, from a distance where they are less open to attack themselves.

A common task of the bishop is to pin potentially-active hostile knights.

As has been observed, the bishop, like the rook and the queen, operates to greater advantage on an open board.

The efficacy of the bishops depends on free diagonals, therefore avoid curtailing their range by obstructive pawn moves.

(e) Knight

Knights are quite at home in the middle-game, and are best posted on advanced squares free from pawn attack.

They are economical in defence, being capable of holding up an assault by considerably superior forces on the king; and very effective in attack, the sacrifice of a knight for a pawn often completely destroying an otherwise impregnable position.

Knights are least effective when guarding one another, since, if both are attacked by a piece, neither can move without loss of the other. They are most effective when working in conjunction on opposite-coloured squares.

(f) Pawn

The pawns are as important in the middle-game as they are in the other stages.

In defence, they present a united front to direct onslaught; the more they are moved the weaker they become as a body creating "holes", or undefended squares, for occupation by enemy pieces.

In attack, the pawns are the battering-rams used to breach the enemy position. A spearhead of pawns, supported by pieces, advancing on a king position stands an infinitely greater chance of success than an attack by pieces alone.

Pawns are well-employed defending pieces from attack by hostile pieces, and they are also the best men with which to attack hostile pieces because of their relatively inferior value.

It must be kept in mind throughout the middle-game that all pawns are potential queens. Try to picture the skeleton when the meat is off, and play for a favourable end-game position before forcing the exchange of too many pieces.

3. The End-Game
(a) King
In the ending the king assumes the role of attacker, and his transitory function is to assist in pawn-promotion.

The versatility of the king at close range allows him to penetrate and decimate weak pawn structures.

Too often, when the end-game is reached, players continue to manoeuvre their few remaining pieces instead of bringing the kings forward.

If the opposing forces still contain three or more pieces, an early advance of the king is likely to prove a self-embarrassment.

(b) Queen
With the reduction in forces, the queen's power augments. If in a bad position in the middle-game, the retention of the queen will at least offer chances of a " perpetual " in the ending, for a lone queen can often force the draw in this manner.

(c) Rook
The rooks, since they are generally the last pieces to

c*

go into action in a game, are most commonly met with in end-games; king, rook and pawns versus king, rook and pawns being by far the most frequent.

A book could well be written on the functions of this piece in the ending alone, but briefly the work of the rook is confined to three fields:

(i) Restricting the movements of the hostile king.

(ii) " Mopping-up " and obstructing the advance of hostile pawns.

(iii) Protecting friendly pawns advancing to promotion.

A rook on the seventh rank—particularly if the enemy king is still on the eighth—is almost always strong, as in the middle-game.

Two rooks on the seventh with the enemy king on the eighth usually draws by perpetual check against a similar piece-force, even if a pawn or two down.

Whereas an extra pawn in a king and pawn end-game is usually sufficient to win, with rooks on the board the chances favour a draw. Therefore if a pawn or more down in the ending, endeavour to retain a rook on the board.

All these factors should be borne in mind when the middle-game is drawing to a close.

(*d*) *Bishop*

A paramount maxim to remember here is that if each side is left with a bishop and pawns, and the two bishops are on opposite coloured squares, the game is nearly always drawn, even if one side is a pawn or two pawns ahead.

If a disadvantageous end-game is foreshadowed, play to obtain bishops of opposite colours.

With bishops on squares of the same colour, however,

even a small advantage on one side is usually sufficient to win.

The reason for this is that, with bishops of opposite colours, the play of each side tends to be canalised on to the squares of the same colour as the respective bishops, leaving one party playing on the black squares and the other party operating on the white, thereby creating a deadlock. With bishops operating on the same coloured squares, force will be met by force, and an impasse is unlikely to occur.

Another important fact to remember in the ending is that K, B and RP versus bare K is a draw where the bishop stands on a square the opposite colour to the pawn's promotion square; always provided that the solitary king can get in front of the advancing pawn. As in K and RP versus K, the superior force is compelled to surrender the pawn (leaving insufficient mating force) or give stalemate.

With a bishop on the same-colour square as the promotion square, the stronger side always wins in this type of ending.

Bishops can be employed to good purpose preventing hostile pawn advances. For example, a white bishop on KB1 prevents the advance of any pawn in a black pawn chain extending from KB7 to K6, Q5, QB4, and QKt3. This is an elaborate case, but it demonstrates the power of the bishop in the end-game.

If, in an ending, you are left with a bishop and pawns, the pawns should be advanced to squares of the *opposite* colour to that on which the bishop stands.

This may appear strange, since the bishop cannot then guard the pawns, but this drawback is outweighed by the bishop's greatly increased mobility, and the elimination of duplicated square control. It is quite a common sight to see a bishop reduced to the role of a pawn when the men stand on the squares of one colour.

(e) *Knight*

In the ending the powers of the knight are limited, owing to the comparative impotence of its march on a free board.

A player left with knight and pawns against a bishop and pawns should, if possible, force off by exchanges the pawns on one side of the board, as the knight is seriously handicapped in having to watch both wings. The converse, of course, holds good—if left with a bishop and pawns against a knight and pawns, essay to keep pawns on both wings, on which the bishop, with its greater powers, is able to operate simultaneously.

(f) *Pawn*

When one talks of the end-game one is really discussing pawns, and their handling is therefore of the utmost importance.

Their play is examined at length in the chapter on the end-game; it suffices here to quote a few general rules.

When there is a choice of pawn moves in the ending, the one that is farthest from the scene of operations (usually centred around the kings) should be made.

Remember always that a rook's pawn is insufficient to win, other things being equal, therefore pawn exchanges must be planned accordingly.

The advance of a pawn can be arrested by the sacrifice of a piece if necessary, a device which should not be overlooked.

In the ending, the remote wing pawns play their part, the centre struggle no longer dominating the game. A king cannot possibly stop two pawns, one advancing on each wing, but he can successfully blockade two centre pawns advancing together.

As with the pieces, a cautionary eye must be kept on the pawns in the middle-game, in order that they may be deployed to the best advantage when the final phase is reached.

Combinations

So much for the general manipulation of the men at the various stages. Let us now see how they can combine effectively. The joint action of two or more men, working to achieve a desired object—to checkmate the opposing king, or capture material—is known as a combination; a sound combination if its purpose cannot be resisted, an unsound combination if there exists a plausible defence.

Combinations are often initialled by a sacrifice, and the destiny of a game is usually decided by the outcome.

There are a number of standard mates which keep occurring in one form or another, the dispersal of the majority of the men being purely incidental to the position.

A player should be able to recognise these positions at once, regardless of the camouflage concealing them.

The following examples are all quite common in practice, and cover the vast majority of actual mating attacks in the middle-game. Be on guard against any and every similar position, however secure it may appear, for a deflective sacrifice, that cannot be declined, may be the prelude to catastrophe.

Mating Combinations

(a) A variation of Fool's mate, involving the sacrifice of a piece, is commonly encountered in play. It can occur in the opening: 1. P-KB4, P-K4. 2. P × P, P-Q3. 3. P × P, B × P. 4. Kt-QB3?, Q-R5 ch. 5. P-KKt3, Q × KtP ch. 6. P × Q, B × P mate. (Diagram 15).

(b) A typical middle-game sacrifice is B × RP ch. on a castled king. A conclusive combination is often possible. In the diagram (16) White wins by: 1. B × P ch., K × B?.

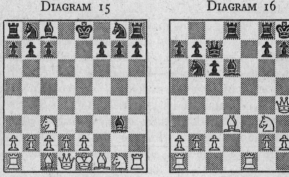

DIAGRAM 15   DIAGRAM 16

EXAMPLE A   EXAMPLE B

2. Q-R5 ch., K-Kt1. 3. Kt-Kt5, R(B1)-K1. 4. Q-R7 ch., K-B1. 5. Q-R8 mate.

(c) After B × RP ch., the most common mating attack begins with B × KBP ch., usually against an uncastled king. Here is a typical example (diagram 17). White wins by: 1. B × P ch., K × B. 2. Kt-K5 dbl. ch. (that fearsome double check again !—the king must move), K-K3 (if 2. . . . K-K1. 3. Q-R5 ch. and mate in two; if 2. . . . K-K2. 3. Kt-Q5 ch.). 3. Q-Kt4 ch., K × Kt (again 3. . . . K-K2. 4. Kt-Q5 ch., etc.). 4. Q-B4 ch., K-Q5 (or 4. . . . K-K3. 5. Q-B5 ch., with mate to follow). 5. B-K3 mate. The forced march of the black king to the centre of the board is typical of this type of attack.

(d) Mate on the back rank by rook or queen is common if the pawns in front of the king have not been moved. In diagram 18 White wins by: 1. R-K8 ch., R × R. 2. R × R ch., R × R. 3. Q × R mate. Be particularly careful of this combination: a decoy sacrifice is very common.

DIAGRAM 17 DIAGRAM 18

EXAMPLE C   EXAMPLE D

(e) An ingenious mating attack, involving a queen sacrifice on the penultimate move, and known as Philidor's Legacy, after a famous French player (diagram 19). White forces mate in five moves: 1. Q-B4 ch., K-R1 (if 1. . . . K-B1?. 2. Q-KB7 mate). 2. Kt-B7 ch., K-Kt1. 3. Kt-R6 dbl. ch., K-R1 (otherwise mate as above: note once again the power of the double check, which White uses to manoeuvre his knight to the desired square). 4. Q-Kt8 ch., R × Q (the king cannot capture as the knight guards the queen). 5. Kt-B7 mate.

(f) Philidor's Legacy demonstrates what is commonly known as a "smothered mate". The description is a good one; all the escape squares for the king being occupied by friendly (?) pieces who stifle the luckless monarch. Smothered mate can only be given by a knight, and is not uncommonly preceded by a sacrifice, as in the previous example. This device can occur in the opening: 1. P-K4, P-K4. 2. Kt-K2, Kt-QB3. 3. QKt-B3, Kt-Q5. 4. P-KKt3, Kt-B6 mate (see diagram 20).

DIAGRAM 19

DIAGRAM 20

EXAMPLE E

EXAMPLE F

(g) A position to be played for if your opponent has castled on the queen's side (diagram 21). White wins

DIAGRAM 21

DIAGRAM 22

EXAMPLE G

EXAMPLE H

quickly by: 1. Q × P ch., P × Q.   2. B-R6 mate.   Note the power of the two bishops working together.

(h) A king behind a fianchettoed position from which the bishop has departed is very weak if the queens are still on the board, particularly if the other player has retained the bishop of the same colour as the Kt2 square and/or a knight.   Examples of this type are for ever recurring, the attacking player basing his strategy on the weakness of the black squares in the king's field (if castled on king's side). In the diagram White wins by: 1. Q-R6 (threatening mate on the move), B-B1.   2. Kt-K7 ch., B × Kt.   3. Q-Kt7 mate.   In this type of position a pawn at B6 is often as good as a bishop; and with a queen established at R6, Kt-B6 ch., followed by Q × RP mate is also a common finale.

(i) A device against a fianchettoed position (normally difficult to attack: diagram 23).   White mates in four by:

DIAGRAM 23

EXAMPLE 1

1. Kt-B6 ch., B × Kt.   2. R × R ch., K-Kt2.   3. B-B8 ch., K moves. 4. B-R6 mate (if 1. . . . K-R1.   2. R × R ch., B-B1.   3. B × B and mate next move).

(j) Another mating position often reached when the bishop has vacated the fianchetto (diagram 24). White

DIAGRAM 24

EXAMPLE J

mates in three by: 1. Q × P ch., K × Q (otherwise mate next move). 2. R-R3 ch., K-Kt1. 3. R-R8 mate.

(k) An end-game attack on a castled king (diagram 25). White mates in three: 1. R-K8 ch., K-R2. 2. B-B5 ch.,

DIAGRAM 25

EXAMPLE K

P-Kt3.   3. R-R8 mate.   The pawn move closes the line of one bishop only to open a line for the other.   All Black's moves are forced.

DIAGRAM 26

EXAMPLE L

(l) With the hostile king in the corner a typical mating set-up starts with a queen sacrifice (diagram 26): 1. Q × P ch., K × Q.   2. R-KR3 mate.

(m) A more unusual position, but nevertheless frequently occurring in one form or another (diagram 27).

DIAGRAM 27

EXAMPLE M

White wins by: 1. R × P ch., R × R. 2. Kt-B6 ch., K-R1. 3. Q-R5 and mate is unavoidable. If 1. . . . K-R1, White can win in a number of ways; for example: 2. Q-Kt2, B-K3. 3. Q-Kt6 and mate next move. Black can only prolong the agony by sacrificing his queen.

Material-Winning Combinations

There exist a number of stereotyped combinations for winning material (i.e. gaining an enemy man or men for nothing, or for the loss of a weaker force) arising from certain positions that are met with time and again in one form or another.

A sound knowledge of these basic positions and how to exploit them will prove of inestimable value to the student.

Three good rules to observe in order to avoid loss of material are:

(1) Watch all checks.

(2) Watch all "discovered" attacks.

(3) Do not leave men undefended or insufficiently defended unless absolutely necessary.

.   .   .   .   .

(a) An attack on the king (a check) may often succeed in winning material out of hand:

(1) It may force the defender to interpose a stronger piece than the man checking, which then captures it.

(2) The checking piece may simultaneously attack an undefended man, or a more valuable man (a knight fork is a good example of this).

(3) The move may uncover ("discover") an attack on another man.

(4) If a piece on each side is attacked, and one can evade the attack by a checking move, then the other piece, still *en prise*, will fall.

(5) The through check, illustrated in diagram 10 (c) on page 37, is yet another means of winning material in this fashion.

An example of (1) taken from play: 1. P-K4, P-QB4. 2. Kt-KB3, P-Q3. 3. Kt-B3, B-Kt5. 4. P-KR3, B × Kt. 5. Q × B, Kt-QR3?. 6. B-Kt5 ch., and the queen must interpose.

To illustrate (2), another example from actual play: 1. P-Q3, P-QB3. 2. Kt-KB3, P-K4. 3. Kt × P, Q-R4 ch., and the undefended knight is captured next move.

A trap in a well-known defence demonstrates the discovered attack (3): 1. P-K4, P-K3. 2. P-Q4, P-Q4. 3. P-K5, P-QB4. 4. Kt-KB3, Kt-QB3. 5. P-B3, Q-Kt3. 6. B-Q3, P × P. 7. P × P, Kt × QP. 8. Kt × Kt—the trap is sprung, Q × Kt? 9. B-Kt5 ch., and the black queen is lost. See diagram 28.

DIAGRAM 28

FINAL POSITION

A game opening will serve to make (4) clear: 1. P-K4, P-QB4. 2. Kt-KB3, P-Q3. 3. B-B4, B-Kt5. 4. Kt-B3, Kt-QB3. 5. P-KR3, B-R4. 6. P-KKt4 (attacking the

bishop again), Kt-R4 (attacking White's bishop).
7. B-Kt5 ch., winning a piece (see diagram 29). These
opening examples given to demonstrate elementary
stratagems are not, of course, intended as patterns of model
play.

DIAGRAM 29

FINAL POSITION

(b) When two undefended men are attacked simultaneously, one is frequently lost. In the diagram (30), the
rook threatens both the knight and the bishop and must
win one of them.

(c) Underprotection. A very common failing of inexperienced players is to use one man to perform two
functions—for example, guarding two pieces. In the
diagram (31), the black king is defending both the knight
and the bishop. White wins a piece by: 1. Kt × Kt, for
if K × Kt, K × B.

(d) Two knights guarding one another are weak. In
the diagram (32) the rook is attacking both knights. The
white bishop is threatening to capture one of them, and
Black must lose a piece.

(e) A similar type of manoeuvre to (a) is the threat of mate combined with the divergent attack on an undefended man. Such a position may occur early in the game. Examine diagram 33, a position which can arise from an opening called the Colle System : Black's previous move (P-Kt3) was bad, and now White threatens Q-R7 mate and Q × R. The mate must be attended to, and the rook is consequently lost.

DIAGRAM 30

DIAGRAM 33

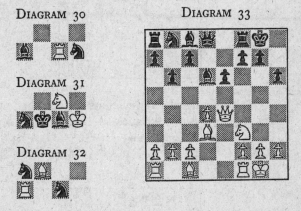

DIAGRAM 31

DIAGRAM 32

(f) The " discovered " attack almost always wins material: 1. P-K4, P-K4. 2. Kt-KB3, Kt-QB3. 3. B-B4, Kt-B3. 4. P-Q3, KKt-R4?. 5. Kt × P (discovering the queen attack on the unprotected knight), Kt × Kt. 6. Q × Kt and White has won a pawn.

(g) A similar device to (f) which wins a pawn: 1. P-K4, P-K3. 2. P-Q4, P-Q4. 3. P-K5, P-QB4. 4. P-QB3, Kt-QB3. 5. KB-Kt5, B-Q2. 6. Kt-B3?, Kt × KP. And now if B × B, Kt × B; and if Kt (or P) × Kt, B × B. This very common trap continues to net a large haul of victims (including quite experienced players) year after year. The diagram (34) gives the position after Black's 6th move.

DIAGRAM 34

(h) A common material-winning device, particularly in the opening, is the advance on a hemmed-in bishop: 1. P-K4, P-QB4. 2. Kt-KB3, Kt-QB3. 3. B-B4, P-Q3. 4. O-O, P-QR3. 5. Q-K2?, P-QKt4. 6. B-Q3 (or

DIAGRAM 35

B-Kt3), P-B5. And White must give up the bishop for two pawns, an exchange we know to be unfavourable.

(i) A pinned man, being immobile, is particularly prone to pawn attack.

DIAGRAM 36

In the opening after, for example, 1. P-QB4, P-K4. 2. Kt-QB3, Kt-QB3. 3. P-K3, Kt-B3. 4. P-Q4, P-Q3. 5. Q-R4, B-B4? White wins a piece for a pawn by: 6. P-Q5, and Black's pinned queen's knight must fall. The diagram (36) shows the position after White's final move.

DIAGRAM 37   DIAGRAM 38

(j) A king may be taken from the defence of a man by a check—very often by a sacrifice. This is also liable to occur in the opening, and a good example is appended. 1. P-K4, P-QB4. 2. Kt-KB3, Kt-QB3. 3. P-Q4, P × P. 4. Kt × P, Kt-B3. 5. Kt-QB3, P-Q3. 6. KB-B4, P-KKt3. 7. Kt × Kt, P × Kt. 8. P-K5, P × P? 9. B × P ch.! (see diagram 37). Now Black must recapture with the king and the queen is lost.

(k) A " forced " move, that is to say, a move that must be made either to save the game or as a matter of legality, may frequently concede material. Diagram 38 shows a very common stratagem. White plays here B-R6, threatening Q × P mate. The bishop cannot be taken as the KtP is pinned, and P-KKt4 would allow mate in two (by Q × P ch., K-R1. Q-Kt7), so P-Kt3 is forced, and now White wins the exchange by B × R

CHAPTER V

THE OPENINGS

Introduction

It has been seen that a game is divided arbitrarily into three phases, the Opening, the Middle-Game and the End-Game. Since an advantage gained in the opening will be carried on into the middle-game, it follows that it is on the opening that the structure and course of the game will immediately depend.

Chess openings have, as might be expected, provided the chief source of research for analysts down the ages. Fortunately no perfect opening has been discovered: the subtleties of a game invented by man transcend man's breadth of knowledge—and seem likely to do so for ever.

Nevertheless, chess scholars have succeeded in determining and classifying the best of the initial moves for both sides to various degrees of profundity. The net result of these years of constant research proves only that there is no proof; that if both players adopt the best lines of play, the game will remain approximately level. Theory is always changing—there are schools of thought in chess as in literature—and what was considered best a hundred years ago is classed as only mediocre to-day. Since analysis is recorded and published, however, the sum of our knowledge of the openings is constantly increasing —not a month passes without new discoveries, of greater or lesser importance, being added to this sum.

Even a quite elementary book on the openings will

bewilder the new player, conveying the impression that chess is a profound, esoteric science rather than a game. Page upon page of continuations, prefaced by exotic names and punctuated with seemingly endless footnotes, each subdividing into further enumerated variations, are enough to frighten the most composed and self-confident of novitiates.

Such works, however, are rarely treated as more than sources of reference ; mentors to indicate the pitfalls that attend the unwary, surgeons to assist the student conducting his own post-mortem.

A good player will follow a book line without being conscious of doing so—simply because his moves are the best in the position with which he is confronted and, in consequence, are listed in the opening compendiums.

The purely " book " player, moving " according to Hoyle ", will find himself at a disadvantage if his opponent deviates from the accepted line.   In order to play the chess openings well, it is not only essential that an elementary knowledge of the recognized or approved lines is acquired, but, more important, that the ideas that activate these lines are clearly understood.   It is all a matter of common sense.

Openings are divided into " open " and " close " games.

Open games are those in which the pieces are developed quickly, and the play is directed chiefly along tactical lines —games commencing: 1. P-K4, P-K4 are mostly in this category; close games are those in which play develops along strategical lines (for example: 1. P-Q4, P-Q4). Broadly speaking, pieces are posted *in front* of the pawns in open games, *behind* the pawns in close games.   Certain openings fall between these two groups and are classed as " half-open ".

This nomenclature is irritating and unnecessary, originally formulated, no doubt, by those who delight in making the simple appear complex, and who believe that everything should be tabulated and pigeon-holed whenever possible.

There are about a score of important openings and several hundred minor and branch openings recognized. In each of these there are variations and sub-variations.

Some of these openings are acknowledged as better than others, but in general choice of opening is dependent purely upon style; a player selecting the line of play (so far as it is in his power to do so) most suited to his temperament.

The majority of openings commence with: 1. P-K4 or 1. P-Q4. Occasionally one of the bishops' pawns is advanced, or a knight brought out first, but never a wing pawn. Openings that begin: 1. P-Q4—the close and half-open games—usually have deep-rooted ideas and involve long-term strategy, and are therefore best avoided in the early stages of a player's development. In this chapter attention will be mainly directed to those openings arising from: 1. P-K4.

All opening theory is based on the control of the centre, the importance of which has already been demonstrated. Control may be effected in three ways:

(1) Occupation—by the establishment of pawns and/or pieces on the centre squares.

(2) Delayed occupation—by permitting the opponent to occupy the centre at first, then attempting to undermine and break up his position.

(3) Remote control—by commanding the centre from a distance by means of the pieces without actually occupying the squares. In this technique one or both bishops are fianchettoed.

Gambits

It is quite common in the opening to sacrifice a pawn (or even occasionally a piece) in order to gain time in development. An opening sacrifice of this nature is called a gambit. There are a number of recognized gambits, the most common being the King's Gambit and the Queen's Gambit, in both of which a pawn is offered.

The question of what normally constitutes a winning force is as important when considering an opening sacrifice as at other stages of the game. Amongst strong players, an extra pawn on one side in the opening, provided other factors—time and space, that together govern position—are equal, is sufficient to win.

With average club players of experience, a minor piece ahead will usually prove decisive. From this it will be seen that a strong player who succeeds in refuting a gambit and obtaining complete equality in position is well on the way to victory.

An Opening (1)

After this superficial survey of opening theory, let us follow an established method of opening, endeavouring to understand the principles underlying the play. The reader may, if he so desire, pass straight on to the next chapter here, returning to the study of the openings after he has mastered the middle- and end-game play. For the sake of continuity the opening is presented before the other two phases; but this is not the best order of instruction.

White	Black
1. P-K4	P-K4

Black could also reply here: 1. . . . P-QB4 (the Sicilian Defence); 1. . . . P-K3 (the French Defence); 1. . . . P-QB3 (the Caro-Kann Defence); 1. . . . Kt-KB3 (Alekhine's Defence; 1. . . . P-Q4 (the Centre Counter), etc. This will give some idea of the variety of play there is even in the very early stages of the game. Each of these defences has its own particular structure and its own band of loyal advocates. Note that after White's initial pawn advance Black is in a position to dictate, to a great extent, the future course of the game.

2. Kt-KB3	Kt-QB3

We have already seen that both of these are good moves.

3. B-B4	B-B4

With the completion of these moves the opening has assumed the extravagant title of the Giuoco Piano. This opening is characterised by the quick development of the pieces and direct and logical assault on the centre. There are no deep-rooted theoretical lines, and it is therefore to be recommended to the student. The two bishop moves maintain the central pressure whilst furthering development.

4. P-B3

Preparing the advance of the queen's pawn.

4.	Kt-B3

Black counters by attacking the undefended KP. To attempt to delay the advance of White's QP by 4. . . . Q-B3, would be bad, as it violates opening principles: (1) It does not assist the development of the minor pieces. (2) It takes away the best square for the king's knight. (3) The queen is vulnerable to attack and time will eventually be lost. White might then continue: 5. P-Q3 (threatening B-Kt5 driving the queen to a bad square) and after: 5. . . .P-KR3. 6. B-K3, P-Q3. 7. QKt-K2, Black would be far behind in development.

5. P-Q4	P × P
6. P × P	

The black bishop is again attacked, and since the queen's pawn is twice protected, capture would only result in the loss of a piece. It will be observed that the White pawn on Q4, referred to here as the QP, is, in reality, the QBP. Pawns, unlike pieces, are always named after the files on which they stand; hence a pawn making a capture, and thereby transferring to an adjacent file, assumes a new title.

6.	B-Kt5 ch.

A check to some purpose, as will be seen. No check should be made just for the pleasure of announcing it; although many think, by some process of muddled reasoning, that such a move, if possible, is always desirable.

7. B-Q2	B × B ch.
8. QKt × B	

Both white knights can recapture the bishop, but this move develops another man. Also, if: 8. KKt × B, QKt × P and Black has won a pawn. If: 8. Q × B, Black replies: 8. . . . KKt × P, again winning a pawn. 8. K × B would be very bad. (1) It would permit Black to play: 8. . . . KKt × P ch. (2) White would thereby surrender the privilege of castling; and (3) the move would not develop a man for the attack.

8.	P-Q4!

Black strikes at the psychological moment. If now:

9. P × P, KKt × P.   10. B × Kt, Q × B; White would be saddled with an isolated centre pawn, difficult to maintain since it cannot be supported by another white pawn, and his powerful bishop would be gone.   Black would be able to continue his development unimpeded, and the balance of Black's B and Kt against White's two Kts would be slightly in the second player's favour.

9. P × P

But White does not care for: 9. B-Q3, P × P.

9.   KKt × P

10. Q-Kt3

Attacking the KKt twice.

10.   QKt-K2

Not: 10. . . . KKt moves.   11. B × P ch., nor: 10. . . . B-K3.   11. Q × KtP.

11. O-O   O-O

Both sides castle king's side, and the position in diagram 39, below, is now reached.   Black has equalised.   On account of White having the first move, the onus is on him to retain the initiative: if Black succeeds in eliminating his opening handicap he is said to have equalised.

DIAGRAM 39

POSITION AFTER BLACK'S 11TH MOVE

Opening (2)

Another example of the Giuoco Piano, in which White gains the ascendency:

White	Black
1. P-K4	P-K4
2. Kt-KB3	Kt-QB3
3. B-B4	B-B4
4. P-B3	Kt-B3
5. P-Q4	P × P
6. P × P	B-Kt5 ch.

So far, the same as the previous example.

7. Kt-B3

White, instead of interposing the bishop (the more passive line), sacrifices a pawn for speedy development.

7.	KKt × P
8. O-O	

White is now threatening Kt × Kt. Note that before castling there was no threat, as the QKt was pinned by the bishop.

8.	B × Kt
9. P-Q5!	

DIAGRAM 40

POSITION AFTER WHITE'S 9TH MOVE

A surprising move. Instead of recapturing the bishop, White attacks another piece. Black has now two pieces attacked simultaneously by pawns. He also has an undefended knight in a precarious position, and, most important, he has not yet had time to castle, so his king remains in considerable danger. To compensate Black remains a piece and a pawn up.

9.   B-R4

Black has a number of moves here, depending on which of his pieces he desires to conserve.

10. P × Kt

White regains his piece, and is now only a pawn down.

10.   O-O

Black castles at the wrong moment. Correct was:
10. . . . KtP × P

11. Q-Q5

A good example of when the queen may be brought out with safety in the opening. Black has two undefended units: the bishop on R4 and the knight. The queen now attacks them both.

11.   Kt-Q3

The only move. Black prepares a counter. If now:
12. Q × B, Kt × B.

12. B-Q3

White now threatens to win a piece with Q × B.

12.   B-Kt3

13. B × P ch.

And here we are at the typical B/Q/Kt attack on the castled king (see Chapter IV, Mating Combinations, example b). Black can only avoid mate by ruinous loss of material. A good sample of an open game; highly tactical, with time as valuable a commodity as force. In a strategical position, a player may make four or five consecutive moves with a knight to post it on a good square, whereas even two such moves in a game of this nature can result in calamity.

Opening (3)

1. P-K4.	P-K4
2. Kt-KB3	Kt-QB3
3. Kt-B3	Kt-B3

Now all four knights are in play and the position is quite solid on both sides. This opening is known as the Four Knights' Game, and since it is lacking in punch—White's third move could hardly be called aggressive as it threatens nothing at all—it is favoured, in general, only by those who like to " play safe ".

4. B-Kt5	B-Kt5
5. O-O	O-O

The development of both sides has been entirely logical up to here. First the four knights came out, then the two free bishops before the queens' pawns are advanced to release the other bishops. Both sides then castled, so that after the advance of the queens' pawns, the queens' knights would not be pinned.

6. P-Q3	P-Q3
7. B-Kt5	

Pinning the king's knight. White is threatening the powerful Kt-Q5 again attacking the KKt.

7.	B × Kt
8. P × B	P-KR3

Attacking the bishop. Black cannot afford to release the knight by moving the queen, since White would then exchange the bishop for the knight, when Black, being compelled to recapture with the Kt's pawn, would be left with a very weak and open king position.

Often in the opening, however, the knight can be unpinned by Q-Q3, a move which allows the recapture with the queen should the knight be captured. This move is not, of course, possible here as Q3 is occupied by a pawn.

9. B-KR4

Maintaining the pin.

9.   Q-K2

Black dare not play P-Kt4 here to release the knight, as his king's position would become very weak. White could sacrifice with advantage: 10. Kt × KtP, P × Kt. 11. B × P, and the knight remains pinned and the black king deprived of all pawn shelter. Since Black did not intend to follow up his attack on the bishop, what, then, was the point of his eighth move since White would obviously not surrender the pin unless forced? This type of position crops up time and again in almost every opening, and its anatomy is worth attention. The move P-KR3 does not lose a tempo, since the bishop is compelled to retire, and its importance lies in that the advance P-Kt4, although not immediately practicable, can be held in reserve to unpin the knight in a single move should the need arise. With the bishop at Kt5 instead of R4 this would not be possible, as the attacker, intent on bigger game, might well be able to afford to leave the bishop at Kt5 following P-KR3, in order just to retain the pin for an extra move. The preventive P-KR3 might therefore be said to be a safety valve in case of future trouble.

10. Q-Q2

A move of manifold purpose. Its merits are worthy of analysis: (a) It prevents, at least for the time being, P-KKt4. Such a blunder on Black's part would meet with condign punishment: 10. . . . P-KKt4?. 11. Kt × KtP, P × Kt. 12. Q × P ch., K-R2. 13. Q × Kt and

White is left with two clear pawns to the good. (b) It neutralises the threatened counter-pin: 10. . . . B-Kt5. (c) It unites the two white rooks, which we know to be desirable. (d) It affords protection for the undefended white pawn on QB3.

The position in diagram 41 has now been reached. An assessment of the game to this point would be favourable to White: (a) He has established an effective pin, forcing a slight weakening of the king's side pawn formation. (b) He has an open file (the QKt file) for his rooks. (c) His position is flexible, an early advance by either the QP or the KBP offering two likely media of attack. (d) He has retained the two bishops. Black, although solidly placed at the present, has no visible attacking prospects.

DIAGRAM 41

POSITION AFTER WHITE'S 10TH MOVE

Opening (4)

The King's Gambit was very popular at the turn of the century, but has been out of favour now for a number of years. This opening provides an excellent example of speedy development of the pieces with small regard for strategical considerations; the play is often wild, and both sides are frequently in peril of sudden collapse.   Here is a typical skirmish:

White	Black.
1. P-K4	P-K4
2. P-KB4	

With this move the character of the opening is established.   Black may now either accept or decline the gambit pawn (the KBP).

| 2. | P × P |

The " King's Gambit Accepted."

3. Kt-KB3

Attacking the centre and preventing: 3. . . . Q-R5 ch. This early knight move is common to almost all openings, and is very rarely inferior.

| 3. | P-KKt4 |

Black supports the pawn on B5.   Notice that this pawn on Kt4 is protected by the queen, hence White cannot now play: 4. Kt × P.   The yolk of White's game in the King's Gambit is the attack against the weak point in the Black defence—KB2.   The surrender of the bishop's pawn opens the file for the white KR (after castling) against this weak point.   In order to keep the bishop's file closed, Black endeavours to maintain the advanced pawn.

4. P-KR4

Hitting at the support.   This is an example of where the advance of a wing pawn in the opening is to be condoned: it is in harmony with the underlying object of the gambit.

| 4. | P-Kt5 |

Black has little option but to advance.   If: 4. . . . P × P, Black's king's side pawns are hopelessly weakened, and neither P-KB3 nor P-KR3, defending the pawns are playable: (a) 4. . . . P-KB3. 5. Kt × P!, P × Kt. 6. Q-R5 ch., K-K2. 7. Q × KtP ch., Kt-KB3 (there is little better). 8. P-K5 and White recovers his piece with a winning attack. (b) 4. . . . P-KR3. 5. P × P, P × P. 6 R × R and wins.

6. Kt-Kt5

This variation is known as the Allgaier Gambit.

6.   P-KR3

The knight is trapped!

7. Kt × P

White has sacrificed a piece to disrupt Black's king's side.

7.   K × Kt

Black has no choice, for the queen and rook are forked by the knight. Although a whole piece to the good, Black is not in an enviable position.

8. P-Q4

Now White's QB attacks the pawn on B4. Observe that White concentrates on speedy development; he cannot afford to permit his advantage in time and space to evaporate by: 8. Q × P, Kt-KB3 (Black gains a move by attacking the queen).

8.   P-Q4

Black must counter-attack quickly or he is lost. This move strikes at the centre and frees the queen's bishop which is now defending the KKtP.

9. B × P   Kt-KB3

9. . . . P × P allows: 10 B-B4 ch., developing the other bishop. Black is aiming to keep the position as closed as possible until he is able to bring his forces into play. If he succeeds in doing this, the extra piece will prove a telling advantage.

10. Kt-B3

Black was threatening: 10. . . . Kt × P

10.   B-Kt5

11. B-K2

White is staking everything on attack. He now prepares to castle, bringing his rook to bear indirectly on the
hostile king. The position now reached is typical of the
opening; there are good chances for both sides in practical
play, when there is the time factor to be considered (in
fact, theoretically lost positions are often won in practise:
time is on the side of the attacker). Notice that Black's
queen's side is still undeveloped, and the king's side of
the board appears to be in complete confusion as far as
the dispersal of pawns and pieces is concerned.

DIAGRAM 42

POSITION AFTER WHITE'S 11TH MOVE

Opening (5)

One of the oldest and most popular openings is the
Ruy Lopez, named after a certain Spanish dignitary of the
16th Century. Recent analysis shows that the Lopez
does not confer the marked advantage to White it was

D*

once thought it did, but no one will assert that the last word has been said on this remarkable opening.

The centre remains the focus of action for both sides, but strategy rather than tactics forms the basis of action.

White	Black
1. P-K4	P-K4
2. Kt-KB3	Kt-QB3
3. B-Kt5	

The strength of this move is not at once apparent, and even its purpose is obscure. It does not pin the black knight as the QP has not moved, and the continuation of B × Kt, QP × B; Kt × P is no threat because of the reply Q-Q5! attacking the knight and king's pawn simultaneously with a good game for Black. The answer to the question as to why the move is made is best answered by the subsequent play.

3.	P-QR3

This is known as the Morphy Defence. Black attacks the bishop immediately with essentially the same idea as in opening (3). Black had several playable lines at his disposal here: 3. . . . Kt-Q5, 3. . . . Kt-B3 and 3. . . . P-Q3 are examples. The text (i.e., the move played) is probably the best, however, as after the retreat of the bishop Black may still adopt any of these continuations.

4. B-R4	Kt-B3

Black develops a piece, attacking White's KP in the process.

5. O-O	

White ignores the attack, sacrificing the pawn for the sake of a gain in tempo.

5.	Kt × P

Black had the choice here of two entirely different lines of play. The text opens the game, promising lively play for both sides. The passive B-K2 would have been more stolid, but on the other hand would not have presented White with any opening difficulties. An excellent example of where players of different temperament and style would demonstrate their preferences.

6. P-Q4

Vigorous play is called for.

6.   P-QKt4

7. B-Kt3   P-Q4

Black counters in the centre—imperative if he is to retain an equal game—and gives back the pawn he won a few moves earlier. This is a most important facet of the sacrifice and one which is frequently overlooked. The player who originally accepted the sacrifice may give back the pawn or piece at the correct moment with gain in time or position. At this point the value of Black's third move (P-KR3) becomes clear. If it had not been played, White could have exchanged the bishop for the knight at the precise point where it would have been to his advantage to do so, and delayed or rendered impossible the advance of Black's QP.

8. P × P

Kt × P is also quite playable here.

8.   B-K3

White was threatening to capture the QP.

9. P-B3

Securing the square Q4, and allowing the KB to be brought into play on the king's side.

9.   B-K2

B-B4 would be bad, as then the black knight on K5 would have had no escape square, for White's KP is attacking both Q3 and KB3.

10. QKt-Q2   O-O

11. Q-K2

Threatening to win a pawn by: 12. Kt × Kt, P × Kt.
13. Q × KP

11.   Kt-B4

A number of inexperienced players would prefer Kt ×
Kt here for Black. Why would such a move be bad?
Because it would exchange off a piece which now has no
immediate use, it would bring White's other bishop into
play thereby uniting the rooks, and, in particular, it would
waste time as the black knight has already taken two moves
to develop. Moves which waste time are always to be
deplored, but in the opening, in which the need for
development is urgent if disaster is to be averted, such
moves are particularly prejudicial.

12. Kt-Q4

With this move, White accomplishes several things.
Firstly he prevents the advance of the black QP, secondly
he attacks Black's QKt, and thirdly he relieves the immobility of the king's side, for now the KBP is free to
advance (with consequent gain in freedom for the rook
behind it), and the QKt has a good square to move to,
releasing the QB in the process. It is pleasing to see how
positions unfold in this manner, each man gracefully
moving into its place in the opening framework.

This would be a good point to leave the game, which is
on the point of entering the middle-game stage. White
is playing for a K-side attack, and his aim is to keep the
centre and the queen's wing closed. Black, on the other
hand, has no chances on the K-side, and will play for a
Q-side attack. Note that Black has the pawn majority
on the queen's wing, White on the king's wing, an align-
ment which is conducive to a two-wing struggle. In the
position, Black's immediate aim is to play P-QB4 as soon

as possible—an objective which will be resisted by White. So long as the QBP remains backward, Black will be unable to assert his superiority on this side. Broadly speaking, White may be said to have kept the advantage of the initial move.

DIAGRAM 43

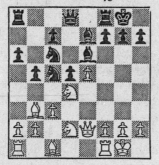

POSITION AFTER WHITE'S 12TH MOVE

Opening (6)

In the 1890's a great American authority wrote that the Queen's Gambit " is now rarely met with in serious play." If he had lived another thirty years he would have seen the opening established as the one most favoured in master tournaments.

Compared with the King's Gambit, the Queen's Gambit is dull in the sense that there is little action in the initial stages. Both sides concentrate on developing their forces, which is accomplished without undue interference.

Because of its complex strategical character, the opening is not recommended to the student, who is advised to concentrate on the KP openings until his knowledge of the fundamentals of play has widened and matured. An opening which has achieved universal acclaim and popularity cannot, however, be ignored, and a typical variation has been selected to give the reader an insight of this type of game.

White	Black
1. P-Q4	P-Q4
2. P-QB4	

The Queen's Gambit. As in the King's Gambit (Opening (4), above), Black may now either decline or accept the proffered pawn ; but whereas in the King's Gambit acceptance of the sacrifice is normal, it is here considered more prudent to decline the offer, at least for the time being.

2.   P-K3

This move shuts in the QB, the development of which is the chief headache for Black in this opening. Black can obviate this handicap by playing here: 2. . . . P-QB3 (the Slav Defence) keeping the diagonal clear for his bishop; but this formation may become very weak when the piece is developed normally on B4 or Kt5. With the text move (the Orthodox Defence) Black retains the option of counter-attacking the centre with P-QB4. If the QP is left unattended, White gains both time and a powerful centre with: 3. P × P, Q × P.   4. Kt-QB3, attacking the queen and following this up with: 5. P-K4. Once P-Q4 has been played, giving control of two of the four central squares, the move P-K4, gaining control of the other two is to be aimed at. The same applies in the K-side openings, where the move P-Q4 is similarly desirable. If the second pawn cannot be maintained the advance is purposeless if not downright bad.

3. Kt-QB3   Kt-KB3

White covets control of the two white squares in the centre (he already controls the black). The QKt attacks both of these, which are again defended by the black KKt.

4. B-Kt5

Pinning the knight, thereby neutralizing its restraining influence on the centre.

4.   QKt-Q2

Setting a trap which has also the merit of developing a piece. If White now continues: 5. P × P, P × P. 6. Kt × P?, Kt × Kt. 7. B × Q, B-Kt5 ch. 8. Q-Q2 (forced, to avoid mate), B × Q ch. 9. K × B, K × B and Black has won a piece. In passing it might be remarked that the springing of opening traps is only desirable if the traps also fulfil some useful function—as in this case. Laying an ambush in the hope that your opponent will fall into it, but accomplishing no other purpose, is a profitless undertaking and one to be avoided, although the temptation is admittedly great at times. One reflects, " What a delightful win I'll pull off if he falls for it ! " and ignoring the pressing demand for straightforward development one embarks on a positionally destructive line of play which is regretted only when it is too late.

5. P-K3   B-K2

White, in playing up the KP, not only freed the KB, but also threatened P × P, as now the king would have an escape square on K2 after the bishop check. Black's reply unpinned the knight, and if now: 6. B × Kt, Kt × B and not B × B, losing a pawn after: 7. P × P, P × P. 8. Kt × P

6. Kt-B3

A quiet developing move asserting White's control of his K5 square.

6.   O-O

7. R-B1

The order of the moves in the Queen's Gambit is frequently of great importance—one of the reasons why it is such a difficult opening to master. The position is pregnant with possibilities and, as is so often the case in chess, the most interesting variations are those which are not played. There is a delicate balance of timing and position which, if upset, spells certain, if protracted defeat. Amongst beginners, who are apt to put men *en prise* at intervals and overlook forced wins, this inexorable punishment of opening misdemeanours is unlikely to occur; but it is, nevertheless, inadvisable to conduct an opening the underlying concepts of which one does not understand.

7.   P-B3

8. B-Q3   P × P

Black correctly waits until the bishop has moved before capturing the pawn, thereby causing White a loss of tempo.

9. B × BP   Kt-Q4

Black must have air for his pieces, and in particular must find a good square for his QB.

10. B × B   Q × B

11. O-O   Kt × Kt

12. R × Kt   P-K4

Black has at last succeeded in playing the freeing P-K4, thereby releasing the bishop; but White is ahead in development.

13. P × P

White decides to dissolve the centre—under the circumstances the most favourable course.

13.   Kt × P
14. Kt × Kt   Q × Kt
15. P-B4

We now come to a position (diagram 44) very commonly reached in the Queen's Gambit. Although White has more pieces in play and a slight pull, Black's position is solid, and with correct play a draw should result. Although the game to this point has been quiet (some players would say dull), the reader should not be deceived into thinking that the Queen's Gambit is a docile, flaccid opening reserved for the mentally bankrupt. Harmless looking positions can explode with alarming suddenness.

DIAGRAM 44

POSITION AFTER WHITE'S 15TH MOVE

Opening (7)

To avoid the cramped positions common to Black in the Queen's Gambit, the defender may adopt one of many good lines in which the second player does not reply to: 1. P-Q4 with 1. . . . P-Q4. The Nimzo-Indian is very popular at present, and a typical variation is given as a mirror of the whole defence.

White	Black
1. P-Q4	Kt-KB3

This is a departure from the normal procedure followed by Black up to this stage of our investigation. Instead of instantly countering the pawn advance, a knight is brought out. Why? It is an effort to evade the rigidity of the Queen's Gambit; Black says, in effect, " I have developed a piece, therefore I have not wasted a tempo, but you do not know what pawn I am going to move." In other words, Black is waiting for White to commit himself to a definite course of action before deciding upon the exact nature of his defence. This spider-and-fly technique has to be carefully handled, otherwise the first player will get an overwhelming game.

| 2. P-QB4 | P-K3 |

Still non-committal. White thinks: Is Black intending to play P-Q4 anyway ?

| 3. Kt-QB3 | B-Kt5 |
| 4. Q-B2 | |

Attacking the important K4 square. White wants to play P-K4 if possible, with a powerful centre pawn formation, and he also does not wish to double his pawns after B × Kt.

| 4. | Kt-QB3 |

In Q-pawn openings generally, the black QBP is moved before the knight. In fact, P-QB4 would be quite good here for Black (as would P-Q4) but, as the sage remarked, " That is another story."

| 5. Kt-B3 | P-Q3 |

Black declares his hand at last: he is aiming at P-K4, a move which White cannot circumvent.

| 6. P-K3 | |

It is interesting to note here that the natural-looking

6. B-Kt5 is bad on account of 6. . . . P-KR3, when if
7. B × Kt, Q × B White has lost a tempo; or 7. B-R4?,
P-KKt4! (quite playable here, as Black has not castled).
8. B-Kt3, P-Kt5, and the KKt must move, when Black
can continue: 9. . . . Kt × P winning a pawn (10. Q-R4
ch., Kt-B3 defends the loose bishop).

   6.   P-K4
   7. P-Q5   B × Kt ch.

If here instead: 7. . . . Kt-K2. 8. Q-R4 ch., wins a
piece, for the bishop at Kt5 is undefended.

   8. Q × B   Kt-K2
   9. Q-B2   P-QR4

Why this curious looking move which, on the surface,
appears a contradiction of our opening principles of centre
development ? It is played to delay the advance of

DIAGRAM 45

POSITION AFTER BLACK'S 9TH MOVE

White's QKtP, for Black intends to bring his KKt to QB4
via Q2 and does not want his piece attacked immediately.
If White now plays: 10. P-QR3, in order to prepare
P-QKt4, Black may continue: 10. . . . P-R5!, and now if

the KtP advances, the black RP will capture it *en passant*. All this subtle manoeuvring is solely to establish a single piece on a good square. Neither side has concentrated on quick development (both kings are still uncastled), and up to here there has been little more than some preliminary sparring. This type of game, which calls for acute strategical judgment, is popular amongst the masters. Again, it is not recommended to the beginner.

Note that no pawns have been exchanged, and the three remaining bishops are all "at home" (see diagram 45). Black has, if anything, slightly the best of it; he will try for a king's side attack, whereas White's chances lie on the queen's side.

Opening (8)

In Opening (1) above, several other defences to White's initial P-K4, other than P-K4 were mentioned. One of these, the Sicilian, is a popular choice of the fighting player; it meets thrust with thrust, counter-thrust with counter-thrust.

White	Black
1. P-K4	P-QB4

Threatening to take off the QP should it advance.

2. Kt-KB3	Kt-QB3
3. P-Q4	P × P
4. Kt × P	Kt-B3

Attacking the KP.

5. Kt-QB3	P-Q3
6. B-K2	P-KKt3

Black intends to fianchetto the KB.

7. B-K3	B-Kt2
8. O-O	O-O
9. Kt-Kt3	B-K3

Both sides are now preparing to attack, White on the king's side (notice those two bishops, and the KBP poised for the assault) Black on the queen's side (Black's KB is indirectly trained on White's rook at QR1).

10. P-B4

Attack !

10.   Kt-QR4

Counter-attack !

11. P-B5   B-B5

12. Kt × Kt   B × B

Not, of course, 12. ... Q × Kt. 13. B × B, winning a piece.

13. Q × B   Q × Kt

14. P-KKt4

White flings caution to the winds; should his attack fail and the majority of the pieces stay on the board, his king's side will prove very difficult to defend.

14.   Kt-Q2

15. Kt-Q5

So far White has had most of the game, and holds a

DIAGRAM 46

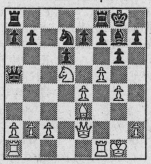

POSITION AFTER WHITE'S 15TH MOVE

decided advantage in position, but Black has plenty of
fight left in the position and the slightest laxity on the part
of the first player will result in a complete change of
fortune.   It is on this razor-blade margin between success
and failure that the appeal of the opening rests; in the
Sicilian, timidity is the precursor of collapse.

Opening (9)

At least as popular as the Sicilian is the French Defence,
which is an ideal opening for the patient player.   Black
allows White to build up a strong pawn centre and then
harasses it, terrier fashion, from van to rear.   As in the
Queen's Gambit, Black's chief worry is the development
of the QB, which is imprisoned by the very first move.

White	Black
1. P-K4	P-K3

It is this move that gives the opening its name.

| 2. P-Q4 | P-Q4 |

These are invariably the second move of each side.

| 3. P-K5 | |

This advance is often delayed.

| 3. | P-QB4 |

Hitting immediately at the support of the K5 pawn:
the tree must be felled by first cutting the roots.

| 4. P-QB3 | Kt-QB3 |

Keeping the pressure on White's QP.

5. Kt-B3	Q-Kt3
6. B-K2	KKt-K2
7. P-QKt3	

The QB must be developed, but White cannot afford to
give up this pawn, which was attacked by the black queen.

| 7. | P × P |

8. P × P   Kt-B4

Black brings his other knight to bear on the QP, which
has now been deprived of its pawn support.

9. B-Kt2

Another man for the defence.

9.   B-Kt5 ch.

10. K-B1

The only move, for if a man is interposed a pawn is
lost. What does our assessment of the position (diagram
47) reveal? Firstly, that so far White has succeeded in
maintaining the pawn at K5—a healthy wedge in the
centre. Secondly, Black has prevented White from

DIAGRAM 47

POSITION AFTER WHITE'S 10TH MOVE

castling whilst retaining a solid defence position himself.
Thirdly, Black has still three pieces trained on the weak
white QP. A factor in White's favour, which is not
evident at first sight, is the mutual embarrassment of the
black KKt and KB. Both can be attacked by pawns, the
knight by P-KKt4, the bishop by P-QR3, and both would
then be best placed at K2. Careful play by Black is
necessary to avoid the loss of a piece.

White will now bring his king to KKt2 after advancing the knight's pawn, and may attack with almost equal facility on either side. Black will rely for defence on the soundness of his position and his pressure on the QP. Note that the second player's game is cramped, and that the QB is as yet undeveloped—two typical features of the defence.

Opening (10)

To turn the wheel full circle, our last opening is theoretically similar to the Giuoco Piano.

White	*Black*
1. P-K4	P-K4
2. Kt-KB3	Kt-QB3
3. P-Q4	

White occupies the centre at once. This mode of continuing is known as the Scotch Opening.

3.	P × P

Observe that P-Q3 would be a strategical error here. 3. . . . P-Q3. 4. P × P, P × P. 5. Q × Q ch., and Black is forced to reply: 5. . . . K × Q, for if 5. . . . Kt × Q, White wins a pawn with: 6. Kt × P. White would therefore have prevented Black from castling.

4. Kt × P	

White could, instead of capturing the pawn, have continued: 4. B-B4 (the Scotch Gambit).

4.	Kt-B3
5. Kt × Kt	KtP × Kt

Not 5. . . . QP × Kt. 6. Q × Q ch., and White again stops Black from castling.

6. B-Q3	P-Q4
7. P-K5	

White does not wish to undouble the black pawns.

7.   Kt-Kt5
8. B-KB4

Defending the attacked pawn and developing a piece.

8.   B-QB4

Black now threatens to win the exchange with Kt × BP, attacking both queen and rook.   That weak KBP again !

9. O-O

Now both the rook and the king guard the weak pawn.

9. . . . Kt × BP.   10. R × Kt, B × R ch.   11. K × B would result in material gain for White.

9.   P-KKt4

White was threatening: 10. P-KR3, driving the knight to a bad square (KR3).   Vigorous counter-action was necessary.

10. B-Kt3   P-KR4

And now Black has a very strong attack.

Notice how weak a bishop is in front of a row of pawns, where it is vulnerable to attack.   Compare this position with a bishop fianchettoed; the KtP at Kt3, the bishop at Kt2, and no sudden attack on the piece by either a knight or a pawn is possible.

DIAGRAM 48

POSITION AFTER BLACK'S 10TH MOVE

Summary

The examples given above are not arranged in any kind of order (sequence is impossible without a starting point), but they are generally representative of their respective openings and run the entire gamut from the patently aggressive (King's Gambit) to the stolidly defensive (French Defence).

But how, the reader asks, am I to assimilate a seemingly endless string of variations, where the first slip may prove dangerous if not fatal ?

Fortunately there is no need to learn more than one or two openings. For example, with the white pieces you will be able to play the English Opening (1. P-QB4) with little fear of your opponent transposing it into another. As Black, in reply to: 1. P-K4, the French, Sicilian or Caro-Kann are three good resources at your disposal, and you can specialise in one of these. After: 1. P-Q4, the Dutch Defence (1. . . . P-KB4) leaves White little option but to follow the normal course of the opening.

If, on the other hand, you open: 1. P-K4 yourself, your opponent will be able to choose his pet defence about which he is likely to know more than you—a factor which will offset the advantage of the move.

However, the adoption of selective lines, based on personal preference of style, should be left until the student has acquired a thorough working knowledge of the theory of the game. Until he is reasonably sure of himself, the advice offered earlier still obtains: 1. P-K4 is the best opening move.

It is said that one cannot ride a horse properly until one has been thrown a few times. The same holds good for chess; more being learned from a few opening debacles than this, or any other chapter could impart.

Major Openings

A short list of the openings commonly met with is given below in alphabetical order. In each example, try to visualise the central pawn structure, the development of the pieces and the strategical aims of each side. It sometimes happens that one opening transposes into another (for example, a Petroff becomes a Four Knights'). Artful transpositions have become a technique of modern master play.

Albin Counter-Gambit. (1. P-Q4, P-Q4. 2. P-QB4, *P-K4*). Black surrenders a pawn for the sake of quick development. Generally good for White.

Alekhine's Defence. (1. P-K4, *Kt-KB3*). Black entices the white pawns to advance, by offering the KKt as a target. He then attacks the advanced pawns which are often weak. Normally slightly favourable to White.

Bird's Opening. (1. *P-KB4*.) An inferior choice for the first player. Can transpose into the King's Gambit. Chances equal.

Bishop's Opening. 1. P-K4, P-K4. 2. *B-B4*.) Can be transposed into several other well-known lines. Has nothing in particular to recommend it, and Black has little difficulty in equalising.

Caro-Kann Defence. (1. P-K4, *P-QB3*.) A popular defence to the King's Pawn, the Caro-Kann is sound but unambitious. It avoids the drawback of the French—the shutting-in of the QB—but has other drawbacks. Slightly favourable to White.

Centre Counter. (1. P-K4, P-Q4.) Black immediately counters in the centre, but after the exchange of pawns his queen is in the middle of the board, and a target for White's minor pieces. Minimal advantage to White.

Centre Game. (1. P-K4, P-K4. 2. *P-Q4*.) White, relying on his extra move, breaks open the centre at once. Equal chances.

Colle System. (1. P-Q4, P-Q4. 2. Kt-KB3, Kt-KB3. 3. P-K3, P-K3. 4. *B-Q3*.) White plans to close the queen's side with P-QB3 and attack on the king's side (by P-K4 etc.). Harmless against careful play by Black.

Danish Gambit. (1. P-K4, P-K4. 2. P-Q4, P × P. 3. *P-QB3*, P × P.) A projection of the centre game, the Danish gives White good chances in practice, due to the free development obtained for the pieces.

Dutch Defence. (1. P-Q4, *P-KB4*.) Black aims at controlling White's K4, and permanently preventing the advance of the KP. The game is usually close in the initial stages. White has slightly the better of it as a rule.

English Opening. (1. P-QB4.) The fianchetto of the KB is normal for the first player. White is often playing the Sicilian Defence with a move in hand but Black has several good lines.

Evans Gambit. (1. P-K4, P-K4. 2. Kt-KB3, Kt-QB3. 3. B-B4, B-B4. 4. *P-QKt4*.) The Evans offers White many compensations for the pawn; a strong centre, quick development and good attacking chances. The refutation, as is often the case with the gambits, consists of giving the pawn back at a convenient moment.

Falkbeer Counter-Gambit. (1. P-K4, P-K4. 2. P-KB4, *P-Q4*.) One of Black's best replies to the King's Gambit. Compare the Albin.

Flank Openings. A whole complex of openings, grouped here under the general heading of Flank Openings, has enjoyed increasing popularity over the past few years. As the description suggests, these openings, are characterised by the avoidance of an early occupation of the centre, at least by one side. The fianchetto of one or more (even all four) bishops is also a feature. The aim is a timely central pawn advance. These openings include the King's Indian Attack, the Pirc, Robatsch and some systems of the English, Reti, and others. A typical Flank Opening might begin: 1. P-K4, P-KKt3; 2. P-Q4, B-Kt2; 3. Kt-QB3, P-Q3. The side which avoids early occupation of the centre must play energetically if he is not to be overwhelmed. Similarly, the side which occupies the centre first must be careful to avoid compromising his pawn structure. Flank Openings should not be played by beginners and straightforward play against these openings is recommended.

Four Knight's Game. (1. P-K4, P-K4. 2. Kt-KB3, Kt-QB3. 3. Kt-B3, *Kt-B3*.) A solid opening, offering little advantage to either side.

French Defence. (1. P-K4, *P-K3*.) One of the commonest replies to P-K4. Both players advance P-Q4, when Black has a secure, but rather restricted position. Popular with positional players who are content to work for an end-game advantage. White usually plays for a king's side attack.

Giuoco Piano. (1. P-K4, P-K4. 2. Kt-KB3, Kt-QB3. 3. B-B4, *B-B4*.) A very old opening in which play is frequently tactical. Sharp attacks by either side are not uncommon. Equal game.

Grunfeld Defence. (1. P-Q4, Kt-KB3. 2. P-QB4, P-KKt3. 3. Kt-QB3, *P-Q4*.) Black tries to exploit the diagonal KR1-QR8 on which White is weak.

King's Indian Defence. (1. P-Q4, Kt-KB3. 2. P-QB4, P-KKt3. 3. Kt-QB3, *B-Kt2*.) Now one of the most popular openings since it gives Black good chances. White usually adopts one of two general systems: a large pawn centre with the king's bishop developed at Q3 or K2, or a less ambitious pawn advance and the KB posted at KKt2. Black sometimes has difficulty in finding good squares for his minor pieces. The King's Indian can easily be transposed into one or other of the Flank Openings.

King's Gambit. (1. P-K4, P-K4. 2. *P-KB4*.) Once one of the most popular openings, the King's Gambit is now rarely seen as White's second move is considered too loosening. The gambit is the starting point of many old and adventurous lines: the Allgaier, Kieseritzky, Muzio are examples. Black may either accept or decline the proffered pawn. In either case he gets an easy game with correct play. The opening is highly tactical.

Max Lange Attack. (1. P-K4, P-K4. 2. Kt-KB3, Kt-QB3. 3. B-B4, B-B4. 4. O-O, Kt-B3. 5. P-Q4, P × P. 6. *P-K5*.) An offshoot of the Giuoco Piano, the Max Lange is packed with attacking possibilities for both sides.

Nimzo-Indian Defence. (1. P-Q4, Kt-KB3. 2. P-QB4, P-K3. 3. Kt-QB3, *B-Kt5*.) A popular and versatile defence in which several different central pawn structures are possible. A positional game in which chances are equal.

Petroff's Defence. (1. P-K4, P-K4. 2. Kt-KB3, *Kt-KB3*.) Black answers the attack on his KP with a counter-attack on White's KP. A sound repy to P-K4, usually good for a draw with best play.

Philidor's Defence. (1. P-K4, P-K4. 2. P-Q4, *P-Q3*.) White gets the more mobile game.

Ponziani's Opening. (1. P-K4, P-K4. 2. Kt-KB3, Kt-QB3. 3. *P-B3*.) An old opening, now considered too slow for the first player. White is aiming at P-Q4, with a strong pawn centre.

Queen's Gambit. (1. P-Q4, P-Q4. 2. *P-QB4*.) Like the King's Gambit, the starting point of several opening systems; for example, the Queen's Gambit Accepted, the Tarrasch, the Catalan, the Cambridge Springs. Very popular until recent years, when the King's Indian and Flank Openings, which avoided an early P-Q4 by Black, came into favour on account of their greater flexibility.

Queen's Indian Defence. (1. P-Q4, Kt-KB3. 2. P-QB4, P-K3. 3. Kt-KB3, *P-QKt3*.) Black aims to control K5 and prevent the advance of White's KP. He therefore fianchettoes the QB.

Queen's Pawn Game. (1. P-Q4). All debuts where White opens: 1. P-Q4, but does not play the Queen's Gambit (through Black's failure to reply: 1. P-Q4, or because White deviates on the second move) are grouped under this heading.

Reti Opening. (1. *Kt-KB3*.). Coupled with P-QB4, P-KKt3 and B-Kt2, the aim of the Reti system is to control the centre without occupation in the initial stages in the hope that Black will set up a rigid pawn structure that will offer targets for attack. A typical Flank Opening (q.v.)

Ruy Lopez. (1. P-K4, P-K4. 2. Kt-KB3, Kt-QB3. 3. B-Kt5). One of the oldest and justifiably most popular of all openings, the Ruy abounds in complex strategical ideas in which the stronger player is likely to come out on top. The opening has several important systems of which two, the Open and Closed systems, are both often played and are widely different in character.

Scotch Gambit. (1. P-K4, P-K4. 2. Kt-KB3, Kt-QB3. 3. P-Q4, P × P. 4. *B-QB4*.) Another attempt by White to get the better of the game by a pawn sacrifice. Black has no trouble in withstanding the attack.

Scotch Game. (1. P-K4, P-K4. 2. Kt-KB3, Kt-QB3. 3. P-Q4, P × P. 4. *Kt × P*.) The opening holds no terrors for the second player.

Sicilian Defence. (1. P-K4, *P-QB4*.) The Sicilian can now be said to be the most popular of all openings partly because of its fighting character and partly because of its seemingly inexhaustible possibilities. It is impossible to set out here the many systems open to both players after the initial moves. Generally White plays an early P-Q4 (when Black exchanges pawns) while the defender himself attempts to play P-Q4 as soon as it is safe to do so. Debacles in this opening are not uncommon, but results are evenly balanced.

Slav Defence. (1. P-Q4, P-Q4. 2. P-QB4, *P-QB3*.) This, and the Semi-Slav. (1. P-Q4, P-Q4. 2. P-QB4, P-K3. 3. Kt-QB3, *P-QB3*.) A resourceful and interesting defence to the Queen's Gambit which is temporarily out of fashion. The Meran system (which either side can avoid) is an exciting variant of the Semi-Slav offering equal chances.

Three Knight's Game. (1. P-K4, P-K4. 2. Kt-KB3, Kt-QB3. 3. *Kt-B3*.) A colourless opening for White. Note that if Black now plays: 3. Kt-B3, the opening has been developed into a Four Knight's.

Two Knight's Defence. (1. P-K4, P-K4. 2. Kt-KB3, Kt-QB3. 3. B-B4, *Kt-B3*.) Interesting play can arise if White immediately attacks the weak KBP by 4. Kt-Kt5. On the whole chances are about even.

Vienna Gambit. (1. P-K4, P-K4. 2. Kt-QB3, Kt-QB3. 3. *P-B4*.) A position can arise not dissimilar to the King's Gambit, with the exception that both QKts are developed.

Vienna Game. (1. P-K4, P-K4. 2. *Kt-QB3*.) A trappy opening in which Black must play with caution. Theoretically, however, the second player has little trouble in equalising and the Vienna is rarely seen in master play.

CHAPTER VI

THE MIDDLE GAME

Introduction

In the Opening and the End-Game the chessplayer can fall back to a considerable extent on the labour of others.

In the Middle-Game, however, he is left on his own. He is like a man in a rowboat who is able to navigate his craft with comparative ease in the regulated waters sidestream, but who is thrown on his own resources when negotiating the main current.

Very little clear-cut instruction can be given on this phase of the game, but there exists an extensive field of theory. A lot of this theory is based on personal preferences, but certain aims, and the means of achieving these aims, are endorsed by all authorities. It is with this field of accepted theory that we are concerned in this chapter.

The Importance of the Centre

A lot has been said already on this subject. Pawns and pieces established on, or controlling, centre squares also exert their influence on both wings.

Pieces, we know, have greater scope when in the middle of the board. A knight posted on a central square can be transferred to any position in two or three moves whereas a knight on the edge of the board would require several moves to reach a vital point on the other wing.

As in warfare, the break-through in the middle is by

E

far the most effective, the defence forces being split into two camps which, being to a degree interdependent, are the more easily destroyed.

A wing attack, even if successful, may not be decisive. In practice, however, the wing attack is the more common because, as a result of the necessity of central concentration in the early stages of the game, a deadlock in this sector frequently ensues.

Exchange of Men

The vexed question of when and when not to exchange has been long encumbered by prejudice and a distorted sense of what constitutes sportsmanship.

Be guided only by the position; if you are ahead in material, endeavour to force exchanges and so increase your strength ratio; if behind, avoid exchanges, particularly of queens, or bishops of opposite colours. Do not let favouritism affect your judgment: many otherwise good players admit to preferences for this or that piece and avoid exchanging even when to do so would be to their advantage. Ignore the widespread belief that exchanging queens early on in the game is a breach of fair play.

Ask yourself the following questions when contemplating an exchange:

(a) Am I ahead in material and well placed for the end-game ?

(b) Which of the two pieces, mine or his, is the stronger or likely to become the stronger ?

(c) Am I losing time by taking his piece off, and would it not be better to let him take mine first ?

Let the answers determine your course of action.

Pawns and Pawn Structures

The importance of the pawn structure is difficult to over-estimate. Pawns can be battering-rams for the attack, bulwarks for the defence; and they can also be grave liabilities in either.

It is in the pawn-play more than in any other sphere that the ineptitude of the beginner is apparent; and yet it need not be so, for the elements of pawn structure are largely a matter of applied logic.

Because of the great influence that pawn formations exert on the middle-game, and to a lesser degree on the opening and end-game, a comprehensive survey of their diverse functions and their merits and demerits are given. Again, generalization has been necessary, and the relative position of the pieces, material and temporal factors must also be taken into account.

Isolated Pawn

A pawn is isolated if there is no friendly pawn on either of the two adjacent files. Because it cannot receive pawn support an isolated pawn is weak.

Doubled Pawns

Pawns are said to be doubled if there are two of the same colour on a file. Doubled pawns are unable to support each other and are particularly vulnerable to attack. Their value is relatively slight (one pawn is able to block two hostile pawns that are doubled). Doubled, isolated pawns are weaker still. Occasionally pawns may be trebled or even quadrupled on a file.

Passed Pawn

A passed pawn is one which is faced with no hostile

pawn either on the same file or on one of the two adjacent files.

A passed pawn is a distinct asset, particularly in the ending, since it will command the attention of an enemy piece to restrain its advance.

Backward Pawn

A backward pawn, as its name implies, is a pawn that has been " left behind " and thereby deprived of its pawn support. It is weak because to all intents and purposes it is isolated.

United Pawns

Pawns standing side by side or supporting one another are said to be united. United pawns are strong.

DIAGRAM 49

Diagram 49 gives examples of the pawn types mentioned. The white pawns on Kt5 and Q2 are isolated. The two black pawns on QKt2 and 3 are isolated and doubled. They are unable to move, being blocked by the single white pawn.

The isolated white pawn on Q2 is a passed pawn, notwithstanding that it has not yet been moved. Black's pawn at KKt2 is backward—it cannot advance without being captured by the white pawn on B5. Both the formations on the king's side are composed of united pawns.

Pawn Formations

A pawn formation is a series of united pawns; it may be mobile or static in character.

(a) **Mobile.** The strongest mobile formation is line abreast, provided the pawns have ample piece support. The attacker then has the option of advancing any pawn, which allows greater flexibility. Two or three pawns are commonly deployed in this fashion, but four or more are unwieldy. The apparent strength of a long line of pawns, often employed by the tyro in a wild attack, is entirely illusory.

(b) **Static.** The strongest static pawn formation is one in the form of a wedge with the apex in the centre, or a single diagonal chain directed towards the centre. The weakest formation is a chain extending outwards from the centre of the board. Diagram 50 will make this clear. The White pawn structure is strong, that of Black weak. White controls by far the greater area. If the men were all moved three squares to the right, however, the position would be reversed, Black having the strong formation and White the weak. The structure is static (none of the pawns can move) and the play would therefore be confined to the pieces. Such formations, it should be stated, are uncommon; but chains of three pawns, as in the last diagram, occur in almost every game at one stage or another.

DIAGRAM 50

United Pawn Structures

Structures of three united pawns are very common, and every combination, together with general remarks on the intrinsic value of each, is classified below. For combinations of four or more pawns, the assessment has only to be extended. Orientations and reflections of a basic structure are not included.

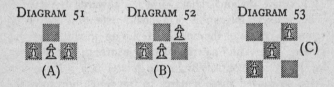

DIAGRAM 51   DIAGRAM 52   DIAGRAM 53

(A)   (B)   (C)

(*A*) Very strong. The pawns command a line of five squares immediately in front of them. If any one is attacked, it may advance one square when it will automatically be defended.

(*B*) Strong, particularly if the advanced pawn is nearest the centre of the board.

(*C*) Strong if the apex is towards the centre, weak if away from the centre. Any bishops remaining on the board must also be taken into account. If White has a bishop on the opposite colour to that on which the pawns stand their value is enhanced; on the other hand, if Black has a bishop on the opposite colour it will detract from the merits of the structure. The reason for this has already been explained in Chapter IV.

DIAGRAM 54   DIAGRAM 55   DIAGRAM 56

(*D*) Strong if combined with a bishop on the opposite colour.

(*E*) Moderately strong if the backward pawn is nearest to the edge of the board, weaker if nearest the middle.

(*F*) Generally weak, but if the centre pawn can be advanced may become strong. The " hole " is an ideal post for a hostile piece.

DIAGRAM 57   DIAGRAM 58   DIAGRAM 59   DIAGRAM 60

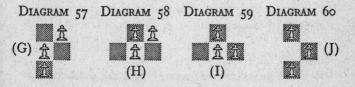

(*G*) Very weak. A single pawn in front of the foremost white pawn can hold the position.

(*H*) Weak, but slightly better if the doubled pawn is away from the centre.

(*I*) Weak, but not so weak as " G " or " H ".

(*J*) Very weak. Again the question of the opposite-coloured bishops will arise.

Pawns in Attack

Supposing Black has castled on the king's side, and the moment is propitious for attack. Which pawn or pawns should White advance ?

The choice usually falls between the KBP and the KRP. It must be remembered that pawns are easily blocked by opposing pawns. It is no good wasting a couple of moves pushing a pawn to the fifth rank if it can then be brought to a standstill without having achieved anything positive.

But a defender will often be compelled to weaken his position to block a hostile pawn, allowing, perhaps, the attacker to make a profitable sacrifice.

The KtP is sometimes advanced to drive away an enemy piece (usually a knight) at KB6, or to attack a RP which has been played to R3 (R6). The attacker must be careful not to expose his own king unless he believes his position to be secure. In this respect the KtP is especially important, as it provides the most shelter for the king.

If an attack with pawns on a castled king is contemplated it is often advisable to castle on the opposite side.

Pawns in Defence

Here we are concerned primarily with the defence of the king after castling, the rules given holding good, however, for defence under most circumstances.

Pawns are at their strongest in their initial positions,

and the golden rule is: " Don't move a pawn until you are forced to." The reason for this is that a pawn once moved offers a target and creates structural weaknesses. The exception to this rule is the advance P-Kt3 in order to fianchetto a bishop. Occasionally a move like P-B4 will block the position, but if this pawn can be attacked by an enemy pawn the measure will only be temporary, and the weaknesses created by the advance may prove to be irreparable.

The defence of the castled king depends to a large extent on the make-up of the attacking forces. Supposing White, who has castled K-side, is under fire from Black. The most vulnerable point is KR2 (compare with KB2 prior to castling), particularly if Black still has his KB (the bishop on the black squares). If he should only have his QB left however, Kt2 is likely to be the focal point of the attack. White must be careful of the move P-KR3 if the black QB is on the board, for the sacrificial B × RP is a very common medium of breaking open a position, since after KtP × B the king has been stripped of his pawn armour.

The main pawn positions that can arise in front of a castled king, together with remarks on the strong and weak points of each, are given in outline:

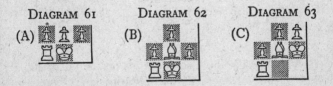

DIAGRAM 61   DIAGRAM 62   DIAGRAM 63

(A)   (B)   (C)

(*A*) Strong; particularly if there is a knight at B3 to guard the RP

E*

(*B*) Strong; particularly if Black has not the same coloured bishop.

(*C*) Quite strong; but not so favourable as the first two. Vulnerable to pawn attack.

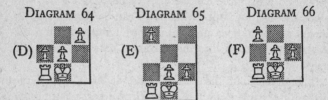

DIAGRAM 64　　DIAGRAM 65　　DIAGRAM 66

(D)　　(E)　　(F)

(*D*) Quite strong if there is also a knight at B3. May be dangerous if Black has retained the bishop that can attack the RP, or if he is able to advance the KKtP with impunity.

(*E*) Strong; particularly if a knight can be brought to B3.

(*F*) Weak, but not unduly so, particularly if P-KB4 can be played in safety.

DIAGRAM 67　　DIAGRAM 68　　DIAGRAM 69

(G)　　(H)　　(I)

(*G*) Very weak if the black queen is on the board supported by one or more of the following : (1) Queen's bishop. (2) One or both knights. (3) A pawn that can be established at B6 or R6 (i.e., either of the holes formed by the advance of the KtP). As has been seen in Chapter

IV, it is not difficult to mate a king in this position. Of course, if the white KB is still on the board and can be brought to Kt2 the position immediately becomes strong (see *B*).

(*H*) Structurally weaker than (*G*), this pawn formation does not, however, offer Black quite so many mating opportunities, but almost any hostile man established at Kt3 will prove a source of embarrassment.

(*I*) Weak. If White has a bishop at Kt2 and a knight at B3 the position is considerably improved. Black's best way of storming this position is by P-KR4-5, attacking the KtP and threatening by exchange to open the R-file.

General

All other pawn formations in front of a castled king are bad; if the rook has been moved away, each position is proportionately worse. The criterion in all the examples, and in (*G*) and (*H*) in particular, lies in whether Black has adequate force and is sufficiently well placed to carry out an attack. If the end-game is reached the pawn structure, so far as the defence of the king is concerned, is inconsequential.

The Pieces

General handling of the pieces in the middle-game has already been covered. The bishops and rooks need open lines on which to operate; the knights strong central squares immune from pawn attack. Two bishops co-operate well, covering diagonals side by side. Queen and bishop and queen and knight work together harmoniously, as do rook and knight. Two or more pieces exercising the same function on a file, diagonal or rank can be powerful; for example, queen and bishop (the queen in front of the bishop) attacking a square, especially in the field of the enemy king. Also two rooks, rook and queen or two rooks and queen on a file or rank (the queen behind the rook(s) here). As far as the ranks go, the seventh and occasionally the eighth are the only two that come in for consideration, as on these the major pieces are secure from pawn attack.

Strong and Weak Squares

Every move by each side results in a change of square values. Weak squares may, and in all probability will be unavoidably created. A weak square may be said to be a hole in the pawn formation—the result, in the majority of cases, of a backward pawn. This weak square will be a strong point for the other side, and since, by definition, it is immune from pawn attack, it will be an ideal post for a piece. Weak squares may be only temporarily weak, however, and the judgment rests, as always, with the players. Master-play is entirely concerned with the aggravation and exploitation of weak points.

Open and Close Positions

Unlike Draughts, blocked positions are not common in chess, although one wing may become paralysed as the result of the rival pawn formations interlocking.

If it is intended to attack on one side of the board it is sometimes advisable to close the other side in order to forestall any possible counter-attack in that quarter. This can be accomplished only by timely pawn advances, and these usually as a counter to hostile pawn movements.

In the close position in particular the ultimate pawn

skeleton should be considered with regard to the end-game.   Such positions afford more opportunity for precise calculation than open games, as with static or near-static pawn formations the advancing kings will not have to contend with mercurial pawn structures necessitating precautionary diversions.

In close positions any discrepancy in forces is less marked than in open positions.   Some years ago a well-known master, playing in an important match, lost his queen for two minor pieces.   He resigned at once, only to realise a few minutes later that the game was so blocked that, despite the heavy material handicap, the outcome could only have been a draw !

In open games, which can frequently arise from close openings it should be noted, the prestige of the pawn suffers; but often—too often—exchanges result in the game fizzling out and some humble, neglected pawn proving the decisive factor.

Piece Traps

There are several traps for winning material that are forever being sprung.   Like Scholar's Mate they are ageless.   It is consequently well worth while to commit them to memory.*

(*A*) **Knight.**   Be careful to leave an escape square for a knight after playing it to R4, otherwise the advance of a hostile pawn may win it.   The same care should be taken if a knight is on the fifth rank with an enemy pawn behind controlling the two best escape squares.

Example: (i) WHITE: Kt on KR4; Ps on K5, KB2,

---

* The examples given are *basic* structures which must be recognised in game settings and are not of course, game positions complete in themselves.

KKt2. BLACK: Ps on K3, KKt2, KR2. If White plays 1. P-B3?, Black wins the knight by 1. . . . P-Kt4.

(ii) WHITE: Kt on K5; Ps on Q4, K3, KB4. BLACK: K on K1; Kt on K2; Ps on Q4, K5, KB2, KR4. Black wins the knight by 1. . . . P-B3.

(*B*) **Bishop.** The hemming-in of a bishop by pawns is demonstrated in " Material-Winning Stratagems " (example (f), Chapter IV). Another common device is the shutting-in of a bishop that captures an undefended rook's pawn.

Example: WHITE: B on K3. BLACK: R on QB1; Ps on QR2, QKt2, QB2. If White now captures the RP— 1. B × P, Black plays: 1. . . . P-Kt3, shutting in the bishop and threatening R-QR1/R × B. White loses a piece for two pawns.

(*C*) **Rook.** A bishop is often able to shut in a rook, winning the exchange.

Example: WHITE: R on K4; P on QR2. BLACK: B on Q3; Ps on QR4, QKt2. If White now attacks the RP he meets with disaster: 1. R-QR4?, B-Kt5 (now the rook cannot escape). 2. P-R3, P-Kt4, winning the exchange for a pawn.

(*D*) **Queen.** A queen is quite easily trapped if she penetrates too far into enemy territory, particularly if she has only one line of retreat open.

Example: WHITE: Q on QR1. BLACK: K on QB2; R on Q1; B on QKt2; Ps on QR2, QKt3. 1. Q × P?, R-QR1 and the queen cannot escape.

The Seventh Rank

In "Powers of the Chessmen" (Chapter IV) we remarked on the power of the rook on the seventh rank, and we also investigated the potentialities of the discovered check.

A type of position not by any means uncommon illustrates the devastating effect of the combination of these two forces: WHITE: R on K7; B on QR1. BLACK: K on KKt1; Q on QR1; Kts on Q2, KB1; Ps on QR2, QKt2, QB2, KKt2. Here the black queen, apparently secure in the corner, falls along with all Black's queen's side men: 1. R × P ch.!, K-R1 (the only square). 2. R × Kt. dis. ch., K-Kt1 (like the wedding-guest, Black " cannot choose but hear "). 3. R-Kt7 ch. (forcing the king back into the discovered check), K-R1. 4. R × P dis. ch., K-Kt1. 5. R-Kt7 ch., K-R1. 6. R × P dis. ch., K-Kt1. 7. R-Kt7 ch., K-R1. 8. R × P dis. ch., K-Kt1. 9. R × Q.

General Maxims

Before going on to practical examples of middle-game play, a few general maxims will not come amiss.

(a) Watch for forks. To someone not familiar with the moves of the men to the point where action and reaction are subconscious, the fork is a perpetual source of worry, particularly where knights are concerned. Momentary " blindness " also results in casualties from the pawn fork. This accounts, curiously, for a higher relative percentage of victims among more experienced players than the knight fork—possibly because the players are more concerned with strategical considerations and are inclined to overlook the anti-positional move. Quite recently two of the world's leading players completely missed a simple fork in an important match. A good moral can be drawn here: keep the play in the right perspective !

(b) Watch the back rank. This warning would bear repetition. Even if no immediate danger threatens, a

" hole " for the king by moving up a pawn is always a sound investment if time and position permit.

(c) Do not attack undefended pieces for the privilege of driving them to better squares. Such pieces are best left " hanging " as they may become ideal targets for combinations at a later stage.

(d) After castling K-side be careful of advancing the bishop's pawn if the hostile king's bishop can check. There is a prosaic finesse winning the exchange which is common to such positions:

WHITE: K on KKt1; Q on Q1; R on KB1; Ps on KB4, KKt2, KR2. BLACK: B on K2; Kt on KKt5 (or K5). White has just played: 1. P-B4?. Play runs: 1. ... B-B4 ch. 2. K-R1, Kt-B7 ch. (forking king and queen). 3. R × Kt, B × R. Black has won a rook for a bishop.

(e) Do not bring rooks into play via R3. Development of this nature is contrary to all elementary precepts, and is invariably bad.

(f) If you intend to attack be careful to keep a fluid pawn formation: do not block the position or allow your opponent to do so.

(g) Finally, remember that in chess timidity pays no dividends—play aggressively !

Examples from Play : (1) King's Side Attack

When discussing the question of an attack with pawns on a castled king it was pointed out that it is often advisable to castle on the opposite side. Here is a good example of this type of game taken from club play. An illustration from master play has deliberately been avoided as the

underlying motives in this class of chess are deep-rooted
and would require extensive annotations to make their
meanings clear to the reader; a course which is undesirable
because it is unprofitable—the wood is more important
than the trees.

	White	Black
1.	P-K4	P-K3
2.	P-Q4	P-Q4
3.	P × P	P × P
4.	B-Q3	Kt-KB3
5.	Kt-K2	B-K2
6.	QKt-B3	P-B3
7.	QB-B4	QB-Kt5
8.	P-B3	B-R4
9.	Q-Q2	QKt-Q2
10.	Kt-Kt3	B-Kt3
11.	Kt-B5	O-O
12.	Kt-K2	R-K1
13.	P-KKt4	

White, having established a strong knight at B5, judges
the moment ripe for assault.   Notice these points :

(a) White's pieces are all in play.

(b) Black's queen's bishop is open to attack from the
advancing pawns.   B × Kt would be a mistake, as
after P × B White would have an open file on which his
rooks could operate against the black king.

(c) White's pawn at B3 completely immobilises
Black's king's knight, for the square K5 would otherwise be an excellent vantage point for this piece affording
chances of counter-attack.

13.   Kt-B1
14. O-O-O   P-QR4

DIAGRAM 70

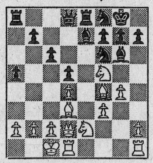

POSITION AFTER BLACK'S 14TH MOVE

Black correctly appraises that his chance now lies in counter-attack on the Q-wing. However, the text move is far too slow and threatens nothing. Vigorous measures were called for, and the correct continuation was: 14. . . . P-B4! threatening to open the QB file for play against the white king. From now on White completely dominates the game.

15. P-KR4

White now threatens P-R5, which would force Black to take off the knight as the bishop has no escape square.

15.   P-KR4

16. Kt(K2)-Kt3

White wishes to recapture at B5 with a knight, and so sacrifices a pawn to achieve this end.

16.   P × P

17. P × P   Kt × P

These exchanges are fatal for Black, who now opens the knight's file as well as allowing the RP to advance.

18. P-R5   B-R2

19. Q-K2   Kt-B3

20. Q-Kt2

White has now gained time and is in a position to capitalise the open file. The immediate threat is the curious Kt × P, and the king cannot recapture because of Kt-B5 dbl. ch., K-R1 and Q-Kt7 mate. The power of the double check is admirably demonstrated: the knight is *en prise* to the bishop and there are three separate pieces which Black can interpose between the king and the enemy queen. But a double check prescribes a king move and nothing can be done to avert the mate.

20.   Kt-K3

21. B-K5

Indirectly attacking Black's weak KtP.

21.   K-R1

The Black king evades the indirect file attack of the white queen only to walk into the indirect diagonal attack of the white queen's bishop. However, there is little to be done.

22. P-R6   P-Kt3

To avoid the opening of the R-file as well, which would be instantly disastrous, Black is compelled to advance the KtP. Now, however, the knight at B3 is pinned, and Black cannot escape the loss of a piece.

23. Kt × B   Q × Kt

24. R(Q1)-B1   K-Kt1

| 25. R × Kt | Kt-B1 |
| 26. Kt-R5 | Kt-Q2 |

Black cannot capture the knight as the pawn is pinned.

27. B × P.

A typical example of bulldozer tactics to crush a weak king's position. Black's last defences are stripped, and in positions of this nature material values lose their significance.

27.	P × B
28. R × P ch.	B × R
29. Q × B ch.	K-B1
30. B-Kt7 ch.	K-Kt1
31. P-R7 mate	

DIAGRAM 71

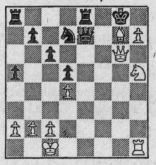

FINAL POSITION

It would be hard to find a more clear-cut example of an attack on a castled king than the foregoing.

It would be a mistake to assume, however, that success in analogous positions would be as swift or as convincing

—or, indeed, that success would necessarily attend the attacker at all. For in the above game Black waited passively for White to gather his strength when he should have himself been active on the other wing.

Apart from this there is little comment to pass; Black, due to his cramped position, could not manoeuvre his pieces effectively—his QR remained unmoved at the end.

One lesson at least may be drawn: it never pays to adopt wait-and-see tactics in the middle-game.

Examples from Play : (2) The Switch Attack

When engaged in a struggle on one wing, an eye should be kept on the possibility of a quick switch-over to the other wing if the opportunity presents itself. Elastic generalship results in fewer missed chances and allows a more comprehensive conception of the changing game-pattern.

Here is another game, taken from County play, in which White never for one moment loses sight of the whole board.

White	Black
1. P-K4	P-K4
2. Kt-KB3	Kt-QB3
3. B-Kt5	P-QR3
4. B-R4	Kt-B3
5. O-O	Kt × P
6. P-Q4	P-QKt4
7. B-Kt3	P-Q4
8. P × P	B-K3
9. Q-K2	B-K2
10. R-Q1	

All " book " up to here.

10.	Kt-R4
11. QKt-Q2.	Kt × Kt
12. B × Kt	Kt-B5
13. B × Kt	KtP × B
14. P-QKt3	P × P
15. RP × P	

White has already gained a positional advantage. He has succeeded in isolating Black's QRP, and obtaining an open file for his rook. He is now threatening R × P.

| 15. | Q-B1 |
| 16. R-R5 | |

This square is momentarily safe from bishop attack, and White takes the opportunity of doubling his rooks on the weak pawn.

16.	Q-Kt2
17. KR-R1	QB-B1
18. B-Kt5	

Played to prevent Black castling. If Black plays now: 18. ... P-KB3, White wins quickly by: 19. P × P, and the black bishop is pinned.

DIAGRAM 72

POSITION AFTER WHITE'S 18TH MOVE

18.	B-QKt5
19. R(5)-R4	O-O
20. Q-Q3	B-Q2

A trap. If now: 21. R × P, B-Kt4!, attacking both rook and queen, would win. However, Black did not expect White to walk the proffered plank, and his real intention was to establish his bishop at Kt4, thereby relieving the weak RP, freeing his QR for action on a centre file, and perhaps attempting to exploit White's backward pawn at QB2. Black is completely blind to White's plan, although White's last move coupled with the presence of the two innocent-looking minor pieces on the K-side should have warned him that his opponent was not wholly concerned with what was happening on the Q-wing. The next move comes as a complete surprise.

21. P-B3	B × R

Black can do no better than accept the offer of the exchange; he is already lost.

22. R × B	B-B4

23. R-R4	

The switch-over. White threatens mate on the move by Q × RP.

23.	P-B4

Black has little option. His two alternatives are even worse. (a) 23. .... P-Kt3, permitting B-B6 and a set-up similar to example (h) of Mating Combinations (Chapter IV), when White can force mate in a few moves; (b) 23. .... P-R3, allowing the sacrificial continuation: 24. B × RP! and Black's king's position is hopeless. This second type of position—when the king is denuded of his pawn armour—has also been referred to previously, an

endorsement of how frequently these standard positions
can arise in play.

24. P × P e.p.

White takes the pawn *en passant*. It cannot be recap-
tured without quick loss, as Q × RP ch. is still threatened.

24.	P-Kt3
25. Kt-K5	P-B3
26. Kt × KtP	

As in the previous example, White sacrifices a piece
on Kt3 in order to break open the position. Here it
cannot be taken without mate in two following: (26. . . .
P × Kt.   27. Q × KtP ch., Q-Kt2.   28. Q × Q mate).

26.	R-B2
27. Kt-K5	R-K1
28. Q-Kt3	

28. Kt × R would be a big mistake here.   28. . . . R-K8
ch.   29. Q-B1 (forced), R × Q ch.   30. K × R, Q × Kt
and wins.   Which goes to show that the primary maxim
" Watch the Back Rank " must always be borne in mind
—more so, in fact, when one has a won game and attention
is more likely to be diverted.

| 28. | Q-R2 |

Black cannot well avoid the double check, for K-B1
or K-R1 would be met with decisive checks from the
bishop and knight respectively.

| 29. B-R6 dis. ch. | K-R1 |
| 30. Kt-Kt6 ch. | K-Kt1 |

Black cannot capture the knight.   30. . . . P × Kt
31. B-Kt7 dbl. ch., K-Kt1   32. R-R8 mate

31. Kt-K7 dbl. ch.	K-R1
32. Q-Kt7 ch.	R × Q
33. P × R mate	

DIAGRAM 73

FINAL POSITION

A delightfully conducted attack with an air of finality in its execution.

Examples from Play :

(3) The Centre Break-Through

A break-through in the centre in the early stages of the game is not common, since it can only be achieved when the opposition is disproportionately weak. This example shows condign punishment meted out to a player who sought inspiration in timidity.

White	Black
1. P-QB4	P-K4
2. Kt-KB3	P-K5
3. Kt-Q4	P-Q4
4. P-K3	P-QB4
5. Kt-Kt3	P-Q5
6. P-Q3	

White was worried about being left with backward a QP.

6.	P × QP
7. Q × P	QKt-B3
8. P × P	P × P

Black has already got a passed-pawn in the centre. Can it be held ? If so, White's game is already lost as the pawn exercises a severe restraint over the white minor pieces. White will take at least two moves to bring another piece to bear on the offender (QKt-Q2-B3), and meanwhile the queen is exposed to attack.

9. P-QR3.

White is afraid of Kt-Kt5, because after: 10. Q-K4 ch., B-K3. 11. Kt × P, Q × Kt. 12. Q × Q, Kt-B7 ch. 13. K moves, Kt × Q., Black has won a piece for a pawn. This line is by no means forced however, and the text move is a waste of precious time.

9.	Q-B3
10. QKt-Q2	B-KB4
11. Kt-K4	

This is a mistake, but Black already has command of the centre.

| 11. | Q-K3 |

Pinning the knight, and threatening to win it next move. Observe how White is compelled to tie up his pieces still further to prevent the loss of this piece.

| 12. P-B3 | Kt-B3 |
| 13. Kt-Q2 | |

Since the knight on K4 is unable to move, this means the Kt on Kt3 to Q2. The only move to prolong the struggle, the complete abandoning of the centre (by, for example, B-K2) would have lost quickly.

| 13. | O-O-O |

Black has succeeded in completely tying up the defence. Now he takes his own king away from the centre, at the same time bringing a rook to guard the advanced pawn. White can do nothing about the terrible threat of: 14. ... Kt-K4! attacking the queen and preparing a further advance of the formidable and now secure pawn.

| 14. K-Q1 | |

To unpin the knight.

14.	Kt-K4
15. Q-Kt3	P-Q6
16. Kt × Kt	P × Kt
17. Q-R4	

Paralysis has now set in, and White is reduced to moving his queen again.

| 17. | B-B4 |

Black guards the attacked RP, brings his last minor piece into play, and unites his rooks all at the same time.

| 18. Kt-Kt3 | Kt × KBP |

A sacrifice of this nature can hardly be wrong in such an overwhelming position.

DIAGRAM 74

POSITION AFTER BLACK'S 18TH MOVE

| 19. P × Kt | |

White has no option but to accept: Q-K8 mate was

threatened. Here: 19 B-Q2 was useless: 19. . . . Kt × B.
20. Kt × Kt, B-Kt5 ch. 21. Kt-B3 (not K-B1, Q-K8
and mate), QR-Q1. 22.K-B1 (Q-R5 is no better), B × Kt.
23. P × B, Q-K8 ch. 24. Q-Q1, B-K6 ch., etc.

| 19. | P-Q7 |

The pawn that has been the cause of all White's trouble
is now sacrificed to force the win. The romantic gesture
is in keeping with its role. Whichever white piece
captures (and again there is no option) will pin itself.

| 20. B × P | KR-K1 |

| 21. B-R3 | |

White had to prevent the mate Q-K8.

21.	Q-K7 ch.
22. K-B1	B × B
23. R-K1	Q × R ch!
24. B × Q	R × B ch.
25. K-B2	B-B4 ch.
26. K-B3	R-K6 mate.

A pleasing finish. Note how White's forces were split in
two by the centre thrust and how, until near the end,
neither of the white bishops or rooks had even moved.
In the final position it will be seen that both the centre
files are controlled by the black rooks and both bishops
are occupying the best possible squares relative to the
position, whereas not one of the white men is well placed.

Examples from Play :
(4) The Queen's Side Attack
The Q-side attack differs fundamentally from the
K-side attack in that there is no target. This is only

true in the broad sense, for in effect any weakness constitutes a target; but a weakness in not strictly a weakness
unless it is exploited.   A Q-side attack may be desirable
for one or more of several reasons; it may be because one's
opponent is engaged on a K-side attack and it is essential
to divert his attentions, it may be because the K-side is
either completely blockaded or so barren of possibility as
to offer little or no opportunity to an aggressor, or it may be
because the dispersal of the men is such as to be conducive
to action on this wing.   In the Q-side attack the balance
of pawns engaged is of prime importance.   By early
exchanges it is common to find one player left with three
pawns against two on the Q-side and with, say, three
against four in the centre and on the K-side.   In any case
the policy of the attacker will be governed to a large extent
by the pawn ratio and the pawn structure, for weaknesses
are created primarily by pawns through their inability to
retrace their steps.

The attacker therefore launches his assault with the
intention of exploiting (or creating) a weakness in order
to achieve an advantage in material, space or time.   The
defender is not, as when resisting a K-side offensive,
obliged to compromise his position by directing his efforts
to the protection of a single man, but may launch vigorous
counter measures whenever he deems the moment propitious.*

Therefore the attacker must constantly be on the alert,
and prepared to change his plan at any apparent change
of weaknesses (i.e., when the defender disposes of one
weakness only to create another).

The example appended is from Master play, and I
have selected it purely for its simplicity of idea and

*It is assumed that both players have castled on the K-side.

execution and not because it is in any way a memorable encounter.

White	Black
1. P-Q4	P-Q4
2. P-QB4	P-K3
3. Kt-QB3	Kt-KB3
4. B-Kt5	B-K2
5. P-K3	P-KR3
6. B-R4	O-O
7. R-B1	Kt-K5
8. B × B	Q × B
9. P × P	Kt × Kt

Not, of course, P × P   10. Kt × P!

10. R × Kt	P × P
11. B-Q3	P-QB3
12. Kt-K2	Kt-Q2
13. O-O	Kt-B3
14. Q-Kt1	

Up to here the game has followed fairly well-trodden paths. White now perceives that the K-side is sterile of opportunity, the centre is closed (there is little chance of being able to force P-K4) and the future of the game lies on the Q-wing.

Although White has the pawn minority on this wing (two to three), Black is handicapped by the disposition of his pieces whereas White can manoeuvre freely. The text move prepares the advance of the QKtP.

14.   P-QR4

Temporarily delaying the advance of the pawn.

15. P-QR3   B-Q2

White has succeeded in creating a small weakness in the Black position: either the QKtP or QBP is going to be permanently backward.

16. P-QKt4   P × P

17. P × P   R-R5

Black has obtained compensation in the open rook's file. He now adopts a typical manoeuvre: by moving his rook up to attack an enemy unit he forces a defensive reply which enables him to double his rooks.

18. R-Kt3

Not: 18. P-Kt5, P × P. 19. B × P, R-Kt5. 20. R-Kt3, B × B. 21. R × R, B × Kt. 22. R × P, Q-K5, forcing the exchange of queens and leaving Black with a material advantage; all of which goes to show that subtle resources frequently lurk in the most innocuous-looking positions.

18.   KR-R1

19. P-Kt5   P-KKt3

20. P × P   B × P

Now the black QKtP has been isolated. The QP is also isolated. Black could have avoided both these contingencies by recapturing with the pawn, but then his bishop would have been shut in, a white rook would have been able to occupy the seventh rank and the advance P-QB4 would probably never have been playable.

21. B-Kt5   R-R7

22. Kt-B3   R(7)-R6

23. R-B1   Kt-Kt5

24. R × R   R × R

25. Kt-Q1

Black threatened to give up his knight for three pawns by: 25. . . . Kt × KP. 26. P × Kt, Q × P ch. 27. K-R1, Q × P.

25.   Q-B2

26. P-Kt3

Black threatened to play Q × P ch. White correctly estimates Black's attack to be of little consequence; he has not now time or force sufficient to take advantage of the enfeebled pawn position.

26.   Q-R4

27. B × B   P × B

28. P-R3   Kt-B3

29. R × P

The weak pawn falls, and Black has a lost position. Observe how White is now able to turn the flank and to proceed on a direct drive against the black king.

29.   R-R8

30. Q-Kt8 ch.   K-Kt2

31. Q-K5

31. R × Kt, hoping for: 31. . . . K × R. 32. Q-K5 mate would have been wrong, because of the reply: 31. . . . R × Kt. ch. 32. K-Kt2, Q-K8, and now White has nothing better than to force a perpetual check by: 33. R × BP ch., K × R. 34. Q-B7 ch., K-B3. 35. Q-Q6, ch., etc.

31.   R × Kt ch.

White has not, in effect, sacrificed a piece for the Black knight is pinned and cannot be saved.

DIAGRAM 75

POSITION AFTER WHITE'S 31ST MOVE

32. K-Kt2	Q-Q1
33. R-Q6	Q × R

There is nothing better. If: 33. . . . Q-B2. 34. Q × Kt ch., K-R2. 35. R-Q8 threatens mate on the move and the queen must be given up. Or: 33. . . . Q-K1. 34. Q × Kt ch., K-R2. 35. Q-B3 attacking both rook and QP and winning easily. Note that here: 35. R-Q8?? would be an error of the first magnitude leading to immediate defeat: 35. . . . Q-K5 ch.!. 36. Q-B3 (not P-B3, Q-B7 mate; nor K-R2, Q-R8 mate), R-Kt8 ch.!. 37. K × R, Q × Q with an easy win—which goes to prove that the margin between victory and defeat is not always as wide as it may appear. The time to take real care is when apparent victory is in sight.

34. Q × Q	R-Q7

35. Q-K5

And Black prolonged the game a few more moves to little purpose before resigning.

F

The game, logical throughout, is a lesson in model play on the part of White. He created weaknesses and exploited them sufficiently to win a pawn, and then turned his attention to the compromised defence structure that remained. Even if Black had not gone in for the faulty combination that cost him the game, it would not have been long before White's extra pawn would have made itself felt. The isolated QP would also have been difficult to defend against the combined assault of the White pieces, and the bolder but swifter death was to be preferred to the torture by suffocation which would otherwise have inevitably ensued.

Combinations

To afford practice in assessing positions where it is often possible to force immediate wins, some examples from play are given and the reader is invited to try his skill. In all cases White, to move, wins. No solution is longer than six moves, and the examples are given in order of difficulty. Solutions are given at the end.

DIAGRAM 76	DIAGRAM 77

DIAGRAM 78

DIAGRAM 79

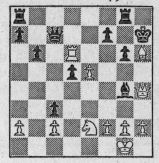

DIAGRAM 80

DIAGRAM 81

Solutions.

DIAGRAM 76: 1. Q × P ch., K × Q. 2. P × P dbl. ch. and mate.

DIAGRAM 77: 1. Q × P ch., K × Q. 2. Kt × P dbl. ch., K-R1. 3. Kt-Kt6 mate.

DIAGRAM 78: 1. Q × P ch., K × Q. 2. B-B3 ch. K-Kt3 (K-Kt1, Kt-R6 mate). 3. Kt-B4 mate.

DIAGRAM 79: 1. B-B8 dis. ch., B-R4. 2. Q × B ch. P × Q. 3. R-R6 mate.

DIAGRAM 80: 1. R-Q8 ch., R × R.   2. Q-R2 ch. (and now White has the Philidor's Legacy), K-R1.   3. Kt-B7 ch., K-Kt1.   4. Kt-R6 dbl. ch., K-R1.   5. Q-Kt8 ch., R × Q.   6. Kt-B7 mate.

DIAGRAM 81: 1. R-R8 ch., K × R.   2. R-R1 ch., K-Kt1.   3. R-R8 ch., K × R.   4. Q-R1 ch., K-Kt1. 5. Q-R7 ch., K-B1.   6. Q-R8 mate.

CHAPTER VII

THE END GAME

Introduction

Very few players can evoke much interest in the end game; it is the calm after the storm, the anti-climax. This is probably why the average player manages it so badly; certain it is that more won games are dissipated in the ending than in the opening and middle-game combined.

There is a tendency to speed up the play when there are only a few men left on the board—and the " obvious " line of play is often the wrong one. The extraordinary subtleties that exist in this branch of the game are prodigious, and seemingly hopeless positions may be redeemed by witch-like manoeuvres. There is an old chess adage that runs, " If you see a good move, look for a better one ", and nowhere does it hold more true than in the end game.

The first prejudice that must be destroyed is that the end game is stereotyped and uninteresting. It demands imagination, patience and accurate calculation. A study of the various piece and pawn endings also accords a valuable insight into the powers, both latent and active, of the individual chessmen.

The Opposition

In order to begin to understand the theory governing the end-game, a clear conception of the " opposition " and what it implies is essential.

If two kings are facing each other on the same file or rank, with one vacant square only between them, the player who HAS NOT the move is said to have the " opposition ". A corollary is the diagonal opposition— two kings standing on the same diagonal with one vacant square between them. Again the player who HAS NOT the move has the opposition.

The opposition is only considered to be in effect if the player who is not possessed of it has no other man except his king that he can move without incurring immediate calamity. If he has a bishop, however, which he can move around at will, the question of the opposition does not arise.

To have the opposition is almost always desirable, and is often a winning advantage for it permits the king to gain territory at the expense of the enemy king, and perhaps, eventually to penetrate the enemy pawn position.

Look at diagram 82. Here the kings are facing each other and the pawn formations are static and to all intents symmetrical. If Black is to move, White wins. If White is to move the game is a draw.

(a) Black to move. 1. . . . K-K3. 2. K-B5 (the white king is at once able to attack Black's pawns), K-K4. 3. K × P, K-Q5 (only now is the black king able to pass to attack the white pawns). 4. K × P, K-K6. 5. P-Kt5, K × P. 6. P-Kt6, K × P. 7. P-Kt7, P-B6. 8. P-Kt8 (Q) and wins.*

*The conclusion requires some care: 8. . . . P-B7; 9. Q-Kt5, K-B5; (9. . . . K-B6? 10. Q × P, P-B8 (Q); 11. Q-KB5 ch., K-K7; 12. Q × Q ch., K × Q; 13. K-Kt5 and the RP queens.) 10. Q-K2, K-Kt6; 11. K-Kt4, K-Kt7; (there is nothing better). 12. Q-Kt4 ch., K-R8; 13. Q-R5 ch., K-Kt8; 14. Q × P ch., and again White can give up the queen for the bishop's pawn, afterwards marching the QRP to promotion. There are other ways of winning this ending.

DIAGRAM 82

Supposing if, instead of: 1. . . . K-K3, Black had played: 1. . . . K-B3. Now White's task is easier: 2. K-K5, K-B2 (the diagonal opposition, but now tactical considerations intervene). 3. K-B5, K-Q3. 4. K × P, K-K4. 5. K-R6 and now White promotes the KtP and wins quickly. Note that the White king *in advance* and *to one side* of the passed pawn assures its promotion. Black can do nothing; viz: 5. . . . K-B3. 6. P-Kt5 ch., K-B2. 7. K-R7 (preventing the black king occupying the promotion square), K-B1. 8. P-Kt6, K-K2. 9. P-Kt7, K-B2. 10. P-Kt8 (Q) ch.

(b) White to move. 1. K-K4, K-K3. 2. K-Q4, K-Q3 and the white king cannot pass, and draw will result by repetition of moves (see Chapter I).

Now remove the four pawns on the king's side and study the position again. What result with each player to move? Answer—as before: White to move, draws; Black to move, White wins.

(a) Black to move. 1. . . . K-B3 (Black has lost the opposition). 2. K-K5 (Why does White make this anomalous move when he could have taken up the diagonal opposition by: 2. K-K4 ?   Because he is able to penetrate the fifth rank on which Black's undefended pawn stands. To have taken the diagonal opposition would only have resulted in maintaining the status quo), K-B2.   3. K-Q5, K-Kt3 (now we see the importance of White's move K-K5; Black is compelled to again surrender the opposition in order to protect the undefended knight's pawn which White is threatening to capture in two moves). 4. K-Q6! (White, having gained territory, is once more able to secure the all-important opposition), K-Kt2. 5. K-B5, K-R3.   6. K-B6 (the opposition again: Black is compelled to relinquish his hold on the pawn), K-R2. 7. K × P, K-Kt2.   8. K × P and White has no difficulty in forcing the win.

(b) White to move.   1. K-K4, K-K3.   2. K-Q4, K-Q3; and we have the same crab-like repetition of moves as before, with neither party yielding ground.

Now replace the four pawns on the king's side and remove the four pawns on the queen's side.   Is the result materially affected?   The answer is no—White without the move wins, with the move can only draw.

(a) Black to move.   1. . . . K-K3.   2. K-K4, K-B3 (the best moves are being played for each side).   3. K-Q5 (temporarily surrendering the opposition, but penetrating the same rank as Black's undefended pawn), K-B2. 4. K-K5 (threatening to win the pawn in two moves), K-Kt3.   5. K-K6, K-Kt2.   6. K-B5, K-R3.   7. K-B6, K-R2.   8. K × P, K-Kt2.   9. K × P and wins.

(b) White to move.   1. K-K4, and now Black can take up the opposition again by K-K3, forcing a repetition of moves.   If he tries to advance among the white pawns the game is still only a draw.   1. . . . K-B4.   2. K-B5, K-Q5.   3. K × P, K-Q6.   4. K-R5, K × P.   5. P-Kt5,

K-K7.   6. P-Kt6, P-B6.   7. P-Kt7, P-B7.   8. P-Kt8(Q),
P-B8(Q) and since both sides have a king and queen left,
the game will be drawn (there are certain exceptions to
this rule).

The thoughtful reader will naturally pose the question
here: Why, in a symmetrical position, does White manage
to draw with the move whereas Black loses?

Study diagram 82 again.   It will be seen that the
position is definitely *not* symmetrical; the white king is
abreast of his advanced pawns, the black king one rank
to the rear of his backmost pawns—in other words, the
white king has the advantage in territory.   If both kings
were moved one rank further down the board the game
would be drawn whoever had the move—both kings
must oscillate impotently on their ranks as they cannot
afford to let the rival monarch intrude.   Observe how the
pawns restrict the mobility of the kings in this situation.

King and Pawn v. King

In the K and P v. K ending, the theme is only carried
a stage further.   Turn back to Diagram 11 in Chapter
II.   In example (a) White to move wins by K-B6.   Because of the pawn at Kt7 the black king is not able to take
up the opposition, and must play: 1. . . . K-R2, when
White promptly gains the opposition by K-B7.   It will
be seen, therefore, that this type of ending (K and P v. K)
is no more than a struggle for the opposition, with the odds
on the superior force.   If the pawn is mobile (not so far
advanced) it can be used to gain the opposition by inter-
polating a move at the critical juncture.   This is best
understood by examining a further example in which
more than one pawn is engaged.

WHITE: K on Q4; Ps on QKt2, QKt4, KB4.

BLACK: K on Q3; Ps on QKt4, KB4. White, with the move, now wins, as he is able to assume the opposition by:
1. P-Kt3.

This angling for the opposition is the essence of K and P v. K play, and great care should be taken to decide whether the king or the pawn should be moved at each turn of play.

As might be expected in dealing with such elementals, simple rules have been devised that dispense with the need for the end-game player to think for himself in this particular sphere. Here they are for reference:

(a) K and RP v. K always a draw if the lone king can reach the corner square first, or if he is able to restrict the opposing king in front of the pawn on the rook's file.

(b) If the pawn is advancing level with, or in front of the friendly king, the lone king always draws if he has the opposition. If the pawn (not a RP) can be played to the seventh rank without giving check, it will queen.

(c) A king two squares in front of his pawn will always win, as the interpolation of a pawn move will give him the opposition.

(d) A king one square in front of his pawn will win if he has the opposition.

King and Pawn v. King and Pawn

The various cases of K and P v. K and P are most important as they are forever recurring. We are not concerned with instances where one pawn immediately falls, or marches through to queen several moves before its rival; but those in which the result may be obscure.

(a) If two pawns stand facing each other away from the edge of the board, and both kings are able to approach the opposing pawns, then the side which approaches first will lose if such approach is not from behind.

WHITE: K on KB5; P on Q4. BLACK: K on QKt4; P on Q4. 1. K-K5?, K-B5. 2. K-K6 (White is compelled to unguard the pawn), K × P and wins. If White approaches from behind, however, the result will be a draw: 1. K-K6, K-B3 (not: 1. . . . K-B5?. 2. K-K5 and it is Black who must give up the pawn). 2. K-K5, K-B2. 3. K × P, K-Q2 and Black has got the opposition.

(b) Where each side has a pawn marching through to queen and the promotions are consecutive, the result is usually a draw, but certain cases arise where the side that is able to check first may be able to win. Here is a typical example: WHITE: K on Q2; P on KR5. BLACK: K on Q5; P on QR6. Although Black is able to promote first, White, with the move, wins by virtue of the first check: 1. P-R6, P-R7. 2. P-R7, P-R8(Q). 3. P-R8(Q) ch., K moves. 4. Q × Q and wins.

Arising out of this " first check " is the necessity for attention to all pre-promotion king moves. WHITE: K on KKt7; Ps on QKt2, KR6. BLACK: K on QB7; Ps on QKt6, KR2. 1. K × P, K × P. 2. K-Kt8, K-B6? (this move loses: any other move, except K-R8, drew). 3. P-R7, P-Kt7. 4. P-R8(Q) ch. Now we see the importance of correct king-play. The black king is in check and he will not be able to queen his pawn. 4. . . . K-B7. 5. Q-R7 ch., (the ending is instructive and is therefore given in full; White must play to drive the black king by a series of checks in front of his pawn, permitting the white king to advance to the scene of operations), K-B8. 6. Q-B7 ch., K-Q8. 7. Q-Q6 ch., K-B8. 8. Q-B5 ch., K-Q8. 9. Q-Q4 ch., K-B8. 10. Q-B3 ch., K-Kt8 (the king was forced to move in front of his pawn to defend it: now the white king advances one square). 11. K-B7, K-R7. 12. Q-B2 (pinning the pawn), K-R8 (not K-R6. 13. Q-Kt1, cutting the king off from the eighth rank). 13. Q-R4 ch., K-Kt8. 16. K-K6, K-B8. 15. Q-QB4 ch., K-Q8. 16. Q-Kt3 ch., K-B8. 17. Q-B3 ch., K-Kt1. 18. K-Q5, K-R7. 19. Q-B2 (the same cycle), K-R8. 20. Q-R4 ch., K-Kt8. 21. K-Q4, K-B8. 22. Q-B4 ch., K-Q8. 23. Q-Q3 ch., K-B8. 24. K-B3, P-Kt8(Q). 25. Q-Q2 mate. If: 24. . . . P-Kt8(Kt) ch., Black has insufficient force to draw.

(c) In the foregoing example Black was left with a K and KtP against K and Q and was unable to save the game. If instead the pawn had been on the bishop's file or the rook's file the result would have been a draw, as by threatening to stalemate himself he would not have allowed time for the hostile king to approach.

(i) **Bishop's Pawn.** WHITE: K on KKt7; P on KR7. BLACK: K on Q7; P on QB6. 1. P-R8(Q), P-B7. 2. Q-Q8 ch., K-B6. 3. Q-B7 ch., K-Kt7. 4. Q-Kt6 ch., K-R8. 5. Q-R5 ch., K-Kt8 (Black always threatens to promote the pawn giving White no time to bring his king up). 6. Q-Kt4 ch., K-R8. 7. Q-R3 ch., K-Kt8. 8. Q-Kt3 ch., K-R1! (instead of moving in front of the pawn as he was forced to do in the last example, the black king is able to move into the corner, for now if White plays Q × P, Black is stalemated). 9. Q-B3 ch., K-Kt8. 10. Q-Kt3 ch., K-R1 and clearly White can do nothing but accept the draw.

(ii) **Rook's Pawn.** WHITE: K on KKt7; P on KR7. BLACK: K on QB7; P on QR6. 1. P-R8(Q), P-R7. 2. Q-R2 ch., K-Kt8. 3. Q-Kt1 ch., K-Kt7. 4. Q-B2 ch., K-Kt8. 5. Q-K1 ch.,

K-Kt7. (Not 5 ...K-B7. 6. Q-QR1.) 6. Q-Kt4 ch., K-B8. 7. Q-R3 ch., K-Kt8. 8. Q-Kt3 ch., K-R8 and Black is left without a move. To avoid stalemate White must move his queen away, and there follows the " mixture as before."

A lesson to be learned from the above examples is the method of bringing the queen up the board by a series of progressive checks, which can be done vertically, as in (i), or horizontally, as in (ii).

These are the only three cases of K and P v. K and P endings that are likely to cause you any difficulty. There are certain exceptions, but being rare in practical play they are not worth our investigation here. To recapitulate: in the cases where one side queens first, and the other side then advances his pawn to the seventh rank supported by his king on the seventh or eighth ranks (also the sixth rank in the majority of cases), the game is a draw if the pawn is on a bishop's or rook's file, a win for the stronger force if on any other file—always provided, of course, that the other king cannot immediately influence the play. If the second party can only advance the pawn to the sixth rank on the move following promotion, the game is always won by the first party regardless of the position of the kings.

King and Two Pawns v. King and One

This is nearly always a win for the superior force, but there are, nevertheless, numerous positions in which the game is drawn. The two most common cases are:

(i) The two pawns are on opposite wings with the single pawn facing one of them. Suppose White is the superior force in this case. Then he wins by deserting his solitary wing pawn, moving across to the other side of the board, capturing the black man and queening his remaining pawn; for Black must attend to the unwatched pawn, which will march to queen if not intercepted and captured. Only in unusual cases can the weaker force draw in an ending of this nature.

(ii) The three pawns and two kings are more or less together. It is then simply a question again of the stronger party deserting one of his pawns at the right moment and going for the other, or of exchanging a pawn in order to get a won position in the K and P v. K category.

Diagram 83 illustrates four positions not uncommon in this type of ending.

(a)   DIAGRAM 83   (b)

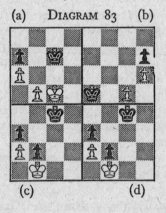

(c)   (d)

(a) Black draws, with or without the move. He has only to keep his king near the pawn. If White advances his KtP, the resulting exchange will leave him with a RP—which, as we know, is insufficient to win.

(b) White wins by an immediate sacrifice, regardless of the position on the board of the white king. 1. P-Kt6!, P × P. 2. P-R7 and queens next move; or: 1. . . . K-B3.

2. P × P and queens the following move, for the pawn on
R6 prevents the black king approaching.

(c) Drawn, regardless of who has the move. White
just moves his king backwards and forwards between Kt1
and B2, and any attempt by Black to interfere with this
movement will result in a stalemate.

(d) This position is essentially the same as (c) except
that it is away from the edge of the board. In this, and
all similar positions, the stronger force wins, with or
without the move. For example: 1. K-Kt2, K-B5.
2. K-B1, K-K5. 3. K-Kt2, K-Q5. 4. K-B1, K-B6.
5. K-Kt2, K-Q7. 6. K-B1, K-Q8. 7. K-Kt2, K × P
and wins.

King and Two Pawns v. King and Two Pawns

This ending, and all endings involving pawns only of
two or more per side, are no more than cumbersome
equations that have not been reduced to the elemental
configurations outlined above. The question of the
opposition is still the all-important factor, but except for
the fact that freedom of movement for the kings is restricted to a degree by the pawn structures, the play
remains the same.

A well-known device, rarely encountered in actual play
however, is the establishment of a passed pawn when each
side has three pawns, line abreast, facing each other.

WHITE: K on KR1; Ps on QR5, QKt5, QB5.
BLACK: K on KR6; Ps on QR2, QKt2, QB2. Although
the black king can now reach the pawns first, White wins
by: 1. P-Kt6!, BP × P. 2. P-R6!, KtP × P. 3. P-B6.
If 2. .... RP × P, the procedure is the same, viz: 2. P-B6,
etc.

King, Minor Piece, Pawn v. King and Minor Piece

The issue at stake here is a simple one: can the pawn be queened? The important point to remember is that the weaker force has only to sacrifice his piece for the pawn to draw. A simple example will show how important it is for the stronger party to keep the pawn mobile in order to retain any winning chances.

WHITE: K on KR1; Kt on QKt1. BLACK: K on KKt6; Kt on KKt4; P on K4. 1. Kt-Q2, K-R6?. 2. Kt-B3, and now 2. . . . Kt × Kt gives stalemate, and any other move allows White to remove the pawn.

Bishops of opposite colours invariably draw in this type of ending, but with bishops of the same colour the stronger side can often force a victory, the method being to drive the opposing bishop from the vital diagonal by offering an exchange at the moment when such an exchange would yield the opposition. If the opposing king is in front of the pawn, however, and cannot be driven away by checks from the bishop, the game is always drawn.

The Kt and P v. B and the B and P v. Kt are the two most interesting—and most common—endings in this category.

In the first case the superior force endeavours to block the bishop diagonal by intervening the knight, and in the second case to force the win by placing the bishop so as to prohibit the knight from approaching the pawn. The power of the bishop over the knight, which is complementary to the knight's power over the bishop, can be seen if a white bishop is placed on K4 and a black knight on KR5. Here the knight is unable to move without being captured, although the bishop, in turn, may not move to any of the squares in the knight's field without being exposed to the same risk. This setting is normally un-favourable to the knight, but under certain conditions it may be advantageous, particularly if the bishop is nearer the edge of the board than the knight.

If there are more pawns on the board the matter be-comes purely an elaboration of the same theme. The reader is advised to turn back to Chapter II for general hints on handling the minor pieces in the ending.

King and Minor Piece v. King and Pawns

With two pawns, this ending is resolved to a case of where the player with the piece will sacrifice it for one pawn in order to be left with the opposition in the ensuing play, thereby assuring the draw.

If the pawns are on opposite sides of the board, or at least separated, the outcome is not difficult to foresee. Two disunited pawns can frequently " squeeze " a bishop: WHITE: K on KR2; Ps on QKt5, KKt6. BLACK: K on KR5; B on K7. White wins by: 1. P-Kt6, B-B6. 2. P-KKt7, B-Q4; and now the advance of either pawn will force the bishop to capture, allowing the other to promote. With a knight instead of the bishop the two-pawn " squeeze " is even easier. These cases are, of course, assuming that the kings cannot affect the play.

If a minor piece is opposed by three pawns, it is usually possible to promote one of the latter with correct play, but there are a number of positions where this ending is only a draw.

Queen and Pawn Endings

In this type of ending the position of the kings is of the utmost importance. If a king is exposed to a series of checks from which he cannot gain sanctuary, the pawn ratio will have no bearing on the game, which will result in a draw.

If, however, the king is able to reach a position in which he is secure from the attentions of the hostile queen, a mobile extra pawn will be sufficient to win, it being escorted to promotion by the queen.

Rook and Pawn Endings

These are by far the most important, as they are the most common form of ending, due, in part, to the normally retarded development of the rooks in the opening and middle-game which enhances their chances of survival.

As has been remarked elsewhere, when both sides have two rooks left the drawing opportunities that present themselves to the side possessed of the inferior pawn position, structurally or numerically, are greater, on an average, than occur when each side has only one rook remaining on the board.

The endings involving single rooks and pawns are much the more usual however, and the strategy they embrace may be applied in measure to the positions involving the weightier force.

The primary features of this ending may be conveniently tabulated for a ready appreciation of the factors embodied.

(a) **Stopping Promotion.** A rook can prevent the promotion of a pawn assisted by a rook by moving onto the same file as the pawn either behind or in front of it. Place a white rook on QKt8, a black rook on KR7 and a black pawn on QKt7. The black pawn cannot move without being captured, and the black rook is unable to leave the seventh rank. Note that the white rook can move up and down the file without in any way relaxing his vigil on the advanced pawn. Now leave the two

black men where they are and place the white rook on
QKt1. Again the black rook cannot leave the rank, but
now Black can play R-QB7, and the white rook is unable
to move along the rank on account of R-B8 followed by
P-Kt8. From this we see that the rook is best employed
behind an enemy pawn. In these two examples the black
rook is badly placed. Now consider the following
position: white rook on QKt1, black rook on QKt1 and
black pawn on QKt7. Here it is Black who retains the
mobility for his piece—the white rook is unable to move
without allowing the promotion of the pawn. If the
white king is able to reach the pawn first it will fall, if the
black king reaches it first the white rook will be lost or
the pawn will be successfully promoted—the unhappy
choice resting with White. This is always assuming that
no extraneous circumstances can affect play—a proviso
that is omnipresent in this as in all other basic endings.
If, in the example just given, the two rooks are interchanged, White's position is immeasurably improved
for similar reasons.

(b) **The Promotion Check.** This may arise out of
the last example given, and should be very carefully
watched. WHITE: K on KKt2; R on QKt8. BLACK:
K on KKt2; R on QKt8; P on QKt7. The white king is
here in the dismal plight of only being able to move backwards and forwards from Kt2 to R2. Any movement to
the third rank loses at once: 1. K-Kt3, R-Kt8 ch., and
promotes next move. A little more subtle is the pitfall:
1. K-B2?, R-KR8!, threatening to promote immediately,
and if: 2. R × P, R-R7 ch. (the " through check ") and
the rook is lost. If, in a position of this nature, it is desired to play the king forward or across the board, both
of the above traps should be borne in mind.

(c) **Rook and Pawn v. Rook.** The convenient rule for this ending is that if the king of the weaker force can reach the promotion square of the pawn the game is drawn; if it can be prevented from reaching it, the game is won by the stronger force. An exception, as always, is the rook's pawn, which in certain positions is only a draw. There is considerable finesse necessary to consummate the promotion, even after the opposing king has been shut off, as the perpetual check remains a recourse for the weaker player which may not be easily discounted.

(d) **Rook v. Pawn(s).** Two important points to be remembered here. Firstly, that two united pawns that are able to reach the sixth rank without capture will win against a rook, provided that the opposing king cannot interfere; and secondly, that a king and single pawn advanced to the fourth rank or beyond, will draw against a rook provided that the other king is unable to interfere. The first case can be easily proven by just setting the pawns up, placing the rook anywhere on the board where it is unable to capture either of the pawns immediately, and then attempting to arrest promotion. One pawn will certainly fall, but the other will reach the eighth rank safely, and the balance (queen v. rook) is then sufficient to achieve victory.

The second rule is as easy to verify as the first, but why the stipulation " advanced to the fourth rank " ? Because, if only on the third rank, the king can be cut off by the rook, the pawn permitted to advance and then attacked and captured before the king can reach it.

Here is an example to clarify the method: WHITE: K on KR8; R on QR1. BLACK: K on KKt3; P on KR4. With Black to move, the fourth rank is attained by K-Kt4, and the game is drawn. But White, to play, wins by:

1. R-R5, P-R5. 2. K-Kt8, P-R6 (if the pawn is not advanced, the white king will eventually return to decide the issue). 3. K-B8, P-R7. 4. R-R1, K-Kt4. 5. R-R1, K-Kt5. 6. R × P and wins. It will be seen that if the black king had been one square nearer he would have been defending the pawn, and the result would have been a draw.

This " cutting off " of the king is an important feature of rook and pawn end-games. An enemy rook ensconced on the seventh (i.e., on the second) rank can be very disturbing if one's king has not left the back rank.

Conclusion

So far we have covered, if very superficially, the entire field of end-game play. Many of the points stressed require elaboration and, in certain cases, qualification, but essentially the fundamentals are there. Few average players know more about this phase of the game than these fundamentals, and many are not even conversant with all of them. Three endings from play are now given which are wholly delightful in concept and execution; they lend weight to the assertion made earlier that both charm and subtlety may be concealed in apparently dull positions.

Examples from Play : (1) Pawn Ending

The position in the diagram, with Black to play, was reached in a match-game between two strong amateurs. Pawns are level, and at first glance it appears as though a draw is the likely result. A closer examination will disclose that there is considerably more play in the position than at first meets the eye.

DIAGRAM 84

BLACK TO PLAY

White	*Black*
1.	P-B5
2. P-K4	

This is forced. If 2. P × P, K × P. 3. K-Kt2, K-K6; and Black will win the KBP, and with it the game. To give up the pawn is equally suicidal: 2. K-Kt2, P × P. 3. K-B1, K-Q5. 4. K-K2, P-R6. 5. P-R3, K-B6. 6. K × P, K × P, winning easily.

Now Black, who was under the impression that he could walk his king in amongst the white pawns, observes that his opponent has an uncompromised pawn majority in the theatre of the board bounded by the king's file and queen's rook file. Every uncompromised pawn majority (i.e., where no pawn is doubled) must yield a passed pawn, hence any such incursion would be fatal. For example: 2. . . . K-Q5. 3. K-Kt4, K-K6. 4. P-Kt4!, K-Q5 (not: 4. . . . P × P?. 5. P-B5, P × P. 6. P-K5 and queens in three moves). 5. P × P, K × P(B4) (P × P would allow 6. K-B5, when the pawn would again go through to queen). 6. K × P, K × P. 7. K takes either pawn, winning.

2.	K-B3
3. K-Kt4	K-Kt3
4. P-KR3	P-R4
5. P-R4	

These pawn moves are important, and are often decisive in pawn endings. White has the opposition, and the black king is forced to move, allowing the king to penetrate. If it had been White's move in this position he would have lost, as he would have been compelled, since his king is unable to move, to advance a pawn, allowing Black to capture and force the win, i.e.: 1. P-K5, P × P. 2. P-Kt4, BP × P. 3. P-B5, P-Kt6. 4. P-B6, P-Kt7. 5. P-B7, P-Kt8(Q). 6. P-B8(Q), Q-Kt8 mate. If instead of: 4. . . . P-R4 Black had played: 4. . . . P-R3, White's reply would have been: 5. P-R3, and not: 5. P-R4??, P-R4; and Black gets the opposition.

| 5. | K-R3 |

Not, of course, K-B3; when: 6. K-R5 followed by K × P would win for White.

6. K-B5

And now it looks as though White is going to force the win.

| 6. | K-R4 |

White must select from several moves here. The interesting pawn sacrifice: 7. P-Kt4, is not quite sound. 7. . . . BP × P (if RP × P, White wins by: 8. P-R5, P-Kt6. 9. P-R6, P-Kt7. 10. P-R7, P-Kt8(Q). 11. P-R8(Q), Q-Kt7 (the only move to stop the threatened mate at R8). 12. Q-K8 ch., K-R3. 13. Q-Kt6 mate). 8. P-B5, P × P. 9. P-K5, P-Kt6. 10. P-K6, P-Kt7 11. P-K7, P-Kt8(Q) ch., winning. The obvious: 7. K-K6 is fatal, as White would then succumb to the same trap that he himself laid: 7. . . . P-Kt5! (the uncom-

promised pawn majority Black holds on the king's side is
set into motion to yield a passed pawn now that the hostile
king is out of range).   8. BP × P ch. (there is nothing
better), K-Kt4; and the black KBP goes through to queen
unimpeded.

White is therefore left with the alternatives of going to
B6, or playing his pawn up to K5.   If he goes to B6, the
game will be drawn, for Black has nothing better than to
go back with his king to R3, and a repetition of moves will
be the result.   Black could not now play: 7. . . . P-Kt4, as,
on account of the position of the white king, White could
play: 8. RP × P ch., K-R3.   9. P-Kt5 ch., K-R4.   10.
P-Kt6, P-R6.   11. P-Kt7, P-R7.   12. P-Kt8(Q), P-R8(Q).
13. Q mates.   Suppose he plays his pawn up to K5,
what happens then ?   Black must capture: 7. . . . P × P,
and White can do no better than recapture: 8. K × P.
Now: 8. . . . P-Kt5 loses for Black.   9. BP × P ch.,
K-Kt4.   10. K-K4, and Black must yield the pawn.
Both sides now have a clear pawn majority on one side of
the board, and neither side can afford to take the initiative
in establishing a passed pawn without conceding the game
to the other player.   One illustration will serve to demonstrate this: 8. . . . K-Kt3.   9. P-Kt4?, BP × P.   10.
K-Q4, K-B3.   11. P-B5, K-K3.   12. K-B4, K-Q2.
13. K-Q4, and now P-Kt5.   14. BP × P, P-B6.   15.
K-K3, P-Kt6 and wins.

In consequence of the foregoing continuations the
actual game was abandoned at this stage as a draw.   An
altogether highly instructive end-game.

Examples from Play : (2) Bishop and Pawns

This example is also from amateur play.   Although
pawns are level the bishops are of the same colour—a

factor which is important, as we have commented that, in endings of this nature, the side possessing even the slightest advantage in position is often able to force the win.

Here the black king is confined to the edge of the board, and White, with considerable ingenuity, is able to exploit this weakness to secure the win.

DIAGRAM 85

BLACK TO PLAY

White	*Black*
1.	P-Kt6

Black has five plausible moves here, all of which lose. The text appears the most promising, for White is unable to play: 2. P × P, on account of P-R7!.

2. B × RP	B-B1

Black cannot play P × P, as after: 3. P-B5, he would be unable to prevent the mate: 4. B-Kt6.

3. B-Kt8

Threatening B-B7 mate.

3.	B-B4

On: 3. . . . . K-Kt3, White would have continued

4. P-R5 ch., K-B4 (or Kt2).   5. B × P and wins, as after:
5. . . . P × P.   6. B × P, Black cannot play B-Q3, as
this would permit: 7. B-Kt1 mate.   It is amusing to note
that after: 3. . . . K-Kt3, White would be ill-advised to
accept the pawn at once: 4. B × P?, P-Kt7.   5. B-K3 ch.,
B-B4.   6. P-R5 ch., K × P.   7. B × B, P-Kt8(Q).
8. B × Q stalemate !

4. B-B7 ch.   B-Kt3
5. B × P
Threatening B-Q2 mate, as the black piece now blocks
the king's flight square.

5.   B-B4
6. B-B7 ch.   B-Kt3
A vicious see-saw.   Compare the example given under
" The Seventh Rank " in the previous chapter.

7. B × P
And now White wins comfortably.

Let us examine the other lines available to Black on
his first move:

(A) 1. . . . P-B6.   This loses quickly.   2. P-B5
(threatening mate by B-K1), B-Q7 (the only move).
3. B-R4 and Black cannot avert the mate at K8.

(B) 1. . . . P-R3.   Now: 2. P-Kt6!, B-B1.   3. P-B5
(B-K1 is again threatened), B × P.   4. B × B, P-Kt6.
5. P-Kt7, P × P.   6. P-Kt8 (Q, R or B) and White
mates next move.

(C) 1. . . . B-Kt2.   2. P-B5, B-B6.   3. B-R4—the
mixture as before.

(D) 1. . . . B-B1.   2. P-B5, B × P (this sacrifice is
forced, as the mate at K1 is again threatened).   3.
B × B, P-Kt6 (if: 3. . . . P-R3, the continuation is:
4. P-Kt6, as in (B) above).   4. B-Q6 (the mating threat

is now B-B7), K-Kt3. 5. B × P and White wins easily by forcing home a Q-side pawn.

An attractive end game.

Examples from Play : (3) Rook and Pawns

As stated previously, this type of ending is by far the most common, and the position in the diagram is as prosaic as one could wish for. In its banality lies its importance, however, for most players, as Black, would be content with a draw, only too glad to avoid the fatigue of aimlessly shifting rooks around for another twenty or thirty moves. This ending was reached in a match between players of international repute, and Black, far from being satisfied with a draw, perceived that by exact play he could force the win. Every move is an object-lesson in timing and precision.

DIAGRAM 86

WHITE TO PLAY

White	Black
1. R-Q7	

Preventing the advance of the black king.

1.   R-Kt6

Cutting off the white king from the defence of the bishop's pawn.

2. R-R7   R-Q6

Black's task is by no means easy. In general a pawn plus in rook and pawn endings is of little importance if the pawns are all on one side of the board and both kings are in their own territories.

3. R-Kt7

White plays at " wait and see."

3.   K-Kt2!

An extraordinary and profound move. White threatened in certain variations to play P-B5 ch., when on P × P (K × P?, R × P ch.) Black would have difficulty in winning, although two pawns to the good, as R and RP v. R, BP and RP is known to be a technical draw.

4. R-R7   P-R4
5. R-R5   R-Q4
6. R-R3

Of course: 6. R × R, P × R would be instantly fatal for White. But after: 6. R-R7, the subsequent play is recondite yet nevertheless convincing: 6. . . . K-Kt3. 7. R-K7 (not P-B5 ch., as Black can now reply with: 7. . . . R × P, nor: 7. K-B3, R-QKt4. 8. K-K4, R-Kt7. 9. P-B5ch., K-B3! arriving at a similar position as in the actual game), R-QKt4. 8. K-B3, R-Kt6 ch. 9. K-B2, P-R5. 10. K-Kt2, R-Kt7 ch. 11. K-R3, R-KB7. 12. K-Kt4, P-B4 ch. 13. K-R3, K-B3 and with the white king temporarily deprived of taking further part in the game, and with both the white rook and KBP *en prise*, Black is left with a simple win.

6.   K-Kt3
7. K-B3   K-B4

8. P-R3   P-R5

An important move, as will be seen.

9. R-Kt3   P-B3

Now Black is able to stand a rook check without yielding ground and can concentrate on the weak RP.

10. R-R3   R-Kt4

White cannot allow his rook to leave the third rank on account of the menace of a black-rook check.

11. R-B3   R-Kt7

Threatening to win immediately by R-QR7 followed by R × P.

12. R-B5 ch.   P-K4

13. P × P   P × P

Now Black has achieved his object of obtaining a passed pawn on the king's file.

14. R-B4

Possibly R-B8 was slightly better here, but the scaffold is already erected.

14.   R-Kt6 ch.

15. K-Kt2   R-Kt6 ch.

16. K-R2

The only move to save the pawn.   And now the black centre pawn is free to advance, and it is important to recall that if this pawn had been on the bishop's file White could have saved the game here.   Black has calculated very deeply.

16.   P-K5

17. R-B8   P-K6

18. R-KR8   R-Kt3

19. R-R5 ch.

Not: 19. R × P, P-K7 winning; nor: 19. R-K8, R-K3. 20. R-B8 ch., K-K5. 21. R-B1, P-K7. 22. R-K1, K-K6.

23. K-Kt1, K-K7.   24. K-B2, R-B3 ch. followed by K × R.

| 19. | R-Kt4 |
| 20. R-R8 | K-B5 |

20. . . . P-K7 would be a grave error, on account of R-K7 winning the pawn and thereby forcing the draw.

21. R × P ch.	K-B6
22. R-R8	P-K7
23. R-K8	

Not: 23. R-B8 ch., K-K5 !.   24. R-K8 ch., R-K4.

23.	R-Kt7 ch.
24. K-R1	R-B7
25. R-B8 ch.	K-Kt6

26. Resigns

There is nothing to be done, as the white rook must keep checking because of Black's impending R-B8 ch. followed by P-K8(Q), and now the black king comes back until the checks are exhausted.   For example: 26. R-Kt8 ch., K-R5.   27. R-R8 ch., K-Kt4.   28. R-Kt8 ch., K-R3. 29. R-R8 ch. (R-Kt1 is still met by R-B8), K-Kt2 and now White's rearguard action is over, and the end is at hand. A more instructive ending it would be difficult to find.

Conclusion

A favourite query of the average chessplayer is—How can I improve my play ?   It is a question the reader will himself be asking sooner or later.   The answer is simple— study the end-game and go on studying the end-game. Practice will not make perfect, but it will go a long way towards perfection—and in the ending the stakes are high !

A few simple positions are given for the student to test his powers. In problems of this nature the phrase "to win" does not mean that analysis of play right up to the final mate is necessarily required, but only up to the point where victory is solely a matter of time. None of the examples are long, but each contains a "twist" that may occur in practical play.

DIAGRAM 87

DIAGRAM 88

WHITE TO PLAY AND DRAW   WHITE TO PLAY AND WIN

DIAGRAM 89

DIAGRAM 90

WHITE TO PLAY AND WIN   WHITE TO PLAY AND WIN

DIAGRAM 91   DIAGRAM 92

WHITE TO PLAY AND WIN   WHITE TO PLAY AND WIN

Solutions

(87) 1. Kt-K6 ch., B × Kt. 2. R-KB2, Q-B2 (Q × R is stalemate). 3. R × Q ch., K × R; and Black cannot win (see " Bishop in Ending," Chapter IV).

(88) 1. P-Kt6, P × P. 2. P-R6! and queens. Not: 2. P × P, K-K2 and Black wins; but 1. P-R6 (threatening P-Kt6) also wins for White.

(89) 1. R-K1!, R-B7 (R × R. 2. P-B8(Q) ch., K-B2. 3. Q-B5 ch., K-Q1. 4. Q-R5 ch., winning the rook, or 3. . . . K-Kt1/2. 4. Q-Kt4 ch., also winning the rook). 2. P-R3! (now Black is left without a waiting move and he is said to be in " zugszwang ". If R-Kt7 or R7, the pawn queens; whilst if the king moves, K-K7 wins), R-B8. 3. R × P, R-B6 (the rook cannot leave the file). 4. R-Q2 ch., K-B1. 5. R-Q5, K-B2. 6. R-B5, R-K6 ch. 7. K-B6 and queens next move.

(90) This is a very old and instructive ending; White, though a pawn down, is able to force the win. 1. P-R6!, K-Kt1 (to stop P-B7). 2. K-Kt1! (the only move; now the black king cannot move or one of the white pawns

will go through to queen. A pawn is compelled to advance), P-B6. 3. K-B2 (it does not matter which of the three pawns is moved, White's strategy remains the same; it is to place the king on the second rank in front of the pawn advanced), P-R6. 4. K-Kt3 (now Black is in zugzwang; he must give up all the pawns in turn, when his king will be forced to move, allowing a white pawn to promote), P-R7. 5. K × RP, P-B7. 6. K-Kt2, P-Kt6. 7. K-B1, P-Kt7 ch. 8. K × BP, P-Kt8(Q) ch. 9. K × Q (and now Black must let a pawn through), K-B2. 10. P-R7, K × P. 11. P-R8(Q) wins.

(91) 1. R-B8 ch., R × R. 2. Q-R7 ch!!, K × Q (K-B2. 3. P × R(Q) dbl. ch., K × Q. 4. Q × Q). 3. P × R(Kt) ch., K-Kt2. 4. Kt × Q, P-B5. 5. Kt-B5 and Black's pawns are decimated.

(92) 1. B-R1 (the only move), K × B. 2. K-B2, P-Kt4. 3. P × P, P-B5. 4. P-Kt6, P-B6. 5. P-Kt7, P-B7. 6. P-Kt8(Q), P-B8(Q). 7. Q-Kt7 ch., Q-B3. 8. Q × Q mate.

CHAPTER VIII

ILLUSTRATIVE GAMES

The six master games that comprise this chapter have been specially selected and annotated by the international authority, Imré Konig.

They have been chosen not so much for their excellence —although a superlative is necessary to describe each example—as for the dominant themes they portray, and the comprehensive field of strategy and tactics they cover. Although the ratio of openings—five K-pawn to one Q-pawn—is unbalanced, the sum picture of the games is a microcosm of the whole, and a practical recapitulation of the earlier chapters.

Game (1)

The strategy in this game is clear-cut, White's superiority in space affording greater manoeuvrability for his pieces.

White	Black
J. R. Capablanca	E. Eliskases
1. P-K4	P-K4
2. Kt-KB3	Kt-QB3
3. B-B4	B-B4

The Giuoco Piano opening, considered, as its name implies, a slow game: it is not very popular in master play.

4. Kt-B3

Another good move here is P-B3, as played in Openings (1) and (2), Chapter V.

4.   Kt-B3
5. P-Q3   P-Q3

Decorous development ! Neither party interferes with the other—yet !

6. B-KKt5   P-KR3

This move is important, as White was threatening Kt-Q5 followed by an exchange of the black KKt, when Black would have been compelled to recapture with the pawn, creating serious structural weaknesses. How else could Black have parried the threat ? By Kt-QR4, attacking the bishop, when White, to avoid the exchange of this useful piece and to prevent disruption of his centre pawns, would have been advised to play B-Kt3, allowing Black: 7. . . . P-B3, forestalling the occupation of Q4 by the hostile QKt (7. . . . Kt × B would be inferior now, as after: 8. RP × Kt, White would have an open file on which to operate).

7. B × Kt   Q × B
8. Kt-Q5   Q-Q1

To guard against Kt × BP ch., winning the exchange. But Black had another resource here: 8. . . . Q-Kt3 with counter threats. White's best move would then have been Q-K2, and after: 9. . . . B-Kt3, Black has slightly the better game. If, instead, White had played the more aggressive: 9. Kt × P ch., he would soon have found himself in trouble: 9. . . . K-Q1 (attacking the knight and forcing the reply). 10. Kt × R, Q × KtP. 11. KR-B1 (Q × P mate was threatened), B-Kt5. 12. P-B3 (to prevent Kt-Q5), B × Kt. 13. Q-Q2, K-Q2. 14. B × P, R × Kt; and Black has two pieces for a rook and a pawn with much the better game.

9. P-B3

White surrendered " the two bishops " (the two bishops

are slightly superior to bishop and knight remember), but gained two tempi in the process; and now he strikes in the centre in order to press home this advantage in time.

9.   Kt-K2

Capablanca, when playing Black against Canal at Carlsbad in 1929, seven years previously, continued: 9. . . . P-QR4 (to prevent the advance of White's Q-side pawns); but the best line seems to be: 9 . . . Kt-R4. 10. P-QKt4, Kt × B. 11. P × B, Kt-R4. 12. P × P, Q × P. 13. P-Q4, Kt-B3. 14. P × P, Kt × P (Dr. Tartakower-Araina, Nice, 1930). 9. . . . B-K3 is bad because of: 10. P-Q4, P × P. 11. P × P, B-Kt5 ch. 12. K-B1!, and although White foregoes with this move the right to castle, his position in the centre is adequate compensation.

10. Kt-K3!

This move presents Black with a difficult problem since on: 10. . . . O-O. 11. P-Q4, P × P. 12. Kt × P, White would achieve command of the centre, and Black would be confronted with the difficult task of freeing his game either by P-Q4 or by P-KB4.

10.   '   B-K3

This move is a mistake, as Capablanca promptly demonstrates.

11. B × B   P × B
12. Q-Kt3

Threatening two pawns.

12.   Q-B1
13. P-Q4   P × P
14. Kt × P   B × Kt
15. P × B

The first phase may be said to be over. Capablanca, by unassuming moves, has achieved a distinct advantage in the centre, and in addition has an open QB-file for his rooks and a well-posted queen in marked contrast to the defensive position of the black queen.

DIAGRAM 93

POSITION AFTER WHITE'S 15TH MOVE

15.	O-O
16. O-O	Q-Q2
17. QR-B1	

If: 17. Q × KtP, KR-Kt1 regains the pawn and occupies the seventh rank.

| 17. | QR-Kt1 |

Now necessary, as White was threatening: 18. Q × KtP, and if then: 18. . . . KR-Kt1. 19. Q × BP.

18. R-B3	P-Q4
19. Q-B2	P-B3

19. . . . Kt-B3 would have given Black more counter-chances after: 20. P × P, P × P. 21 R-B5, Kt × P. 22. Q-Q3, etc.

20. P-K5	R-B5
21. Q-Q1	QR-KB1
22. P-B3	Q-Q1

23. P-KKt3	R(5)-B2
24. P-B4	Kt-B4
25. Kt × Kt	R × Kt
26. P-KR4	

White has a pawn majority on the K-side, whereas Black's majority on the Q-side has been rendered immobile; White controls more of the board than Black, and his pawn position (wedge-shaped, apex in centre) is superior to Black's—small considerations, perhaps, but quite sufficient for Capablanca to forge a win. The text-move prevents: 26 ... P-KKt4, as after: 27. RP × P, P × P. 28. Q-Kt4, followed by K-Kt2 would be favourable for White.

26.	P-KKt3
27. K-Kt2	Q-K2
28. P-R3	

White does not wish the black queen to exercise her nuisance value on the Q-wing.

28.	Q-Kt2
29. R(3)-B3	Q-K2
30. Q-B2	K-Kt2

Black awaits the gathering storm. White threatened 31. P-KKt4, R(4)-B2. 32. Q × P ch.

31. P-KKt4	R(4)-B2
32. K-R3	Q-Q2
33. P-Kt4	R-KKt1
34. R-KKt1	K-R1
35. Q-Q2	

Threatening P-B5.

| 35. | R-R2 |

36. Q-KB2   P-KR4

Lightening White's task, as he requires open files on the K-side to exploit his ascendency.

37. P × P   R × P

If here: 37. . . . P × P. 38. R-Kt5, followed by the concentration of the major pieces on the open file, would be decisive.

38. R-Kt5   Q-R2
39. Q-Kt3   Q-R3
40. Q-Kt4   R-Kt2
41. R-KKt3   K-R2

On: 41. . . . R-R2. 42. R × R, Q × R. 43. Q × Q, P × Q. 44. R-Kt6, R-K2. 45. R-R6 ch. would win. It is very interesting to note that White's sole advantage in this position rests in his slightly superior pawn formation and his equally slight superiority in space; two factors which are none-the-less capable of deciding the outcome.

42. R-Kt2

The object of this move is to bring the rook over to the defence of the RP, and release the queen for action elsewhere. If White plays at once: 42. Q × P, after: 42 . . . R × P ch., he would be none too happy. 42. R × R allows either Q × R or P × R, and again the KP cannot be taken.

42.   K-Kt1
43. K-Kt3   K-R2
44. R-KR2   R-K2

For now White did threaten Q × P.

45. R-R3   K-Kt2

A weak move, but Black's hopes have already faded. After: 45. . . . R-K1. 46. K-B3, R-K2. 47. R-Kt3, R × P. 48. R × P, R × Q. 49. R × Q ch., K × R.

50. R × R White would still have a winning ending.

46. R × R	Q × R
47. Q × Q	P × Q
48. P-B5!	

The break-through.

48.	P × P
49. K-B4	R-K3

If: 49. . . . R-KB2. 50. R-Kt3 ch., K-R3. 51. R-Kt5.

50. K × P	R-Kt3
51. P-K6!	R-Kt5
52. K-K5	R-K5 ch.
53. K-Q6	R × QP
54. R-K3	Resigns

The pawn must go through to queen. For example:
54. . . . K-B1. 55. K-Q7, R-K5. 56. R × R, P × R.
57. P-K7 ch., and wins.

Game (2)

In marked contrast to the preceding game this match
resolves into an animated tactical struggle in which pawns
are sacrificed boldly in order to secure time and space.

White	*Black*
L. Szabo	T. D. van Scheltinga
1. P-K4	P-K4
2. Kt-KB3	Kt-QB3
3. B-B4	B-B4
4. P-B3	Q-K2

The idea of this move is to avoid the complications
arising from: 4. . . . Kt-B3. 5. P-Q4, P × P. 6. P × P,
B-Kt5 ch. 7. Kt-B3, Kt × KP. 8. O-O (see Chapter V,

Opening (2)).   This is, of course, another Giuoco Piano.

5. O-O	P-Q3
6. P-Q4	B-Kt3
7. P-KR3	

White does not relish the pin by: 7. . . . B-Kt5.

7.	Kt-B3
8. R-K1	O-O
9. P-QKt4	

A pawn sacrifice that Black cannot accept: 9. . . . P × P.
10. P × P, Kt × KtP. 11. B-KKt5 followed by P-K5
would be too strong.

9.	P-QR3.

This move not only loses a tempo but weakens the
position seriously. The correct, though rather recondite
continuation here is: 9. . . . K-R1 (to release the KBP,
at present pinned). 10. P-QR4, P-QR3. 11. B-R3, Kt-
KKt1.   12. P-Kt5, Kt-R4. 13. Kt × P?, P-KB3!
14. B × Kt, BP × Kt. 15. B-R2, KP × P. 16. Kt-
Q2, B × P! with an overwhelming attack (T. D. van
Scheltinga—Dr. M. Euwe; Maastricht, 1946). All this
is very advanced theory and is given here for its academic
interest.

10. Kt-R3	K-R1
11. Kt-B2	Kt-Q1

If, instead of this move, Black had carried out his
original idea of playing: 11. . . . Kt-KKt1. 12. Kt-K3,
with the threat of Kt-Q5, would have proved too powerful.
The aim of the text move is to be able to meet: 12. Kt-K3
with P-B3.

12. B-K3	

But White anticipates Black's defence and cleverly

changes his strategy. Now he threatens: 13. P × P, P × P. 14. B × B, demonstrating the weakness of Black's ninth move as Black can no longer reply RP × P with compensatory play on the QR-file.

12.   Kt × P

This is a mistake, although White cannot make immediate capital out of the exposed position of the knight. Black is too far behind in development to take risks of this nature.

13. P × P   P-Q4

Black was clearly relying on this move when he captured the KP.

14. Q × P   Kt × QBP
15. Q-Q3   B × B
16. Kt × B!

This further pawn sacrifice is stronger than: 16. R × B, as after: 16. . . . Kt-R5 Black would have had some counterplay.

16.   Q × KtP

But if now: 16. . . . Kt-R5?. 17. Kt-Q5, Q-Q2. 18. Kt-Kt5! threatening mate, and with a winning attack.

17. QR-B1

Again directed to gaining the Q5 square for the knight.

17.   Kt-Kt4
18. Kt-Kt5   P-KKt3
19. Kt-Q5   Q-R6
20. B × Kt   P × B
21. R-B3   Q-R4

Black dare not take the RP, leaving the queen out of play.

22. P-K6!

DIAGRAM 94

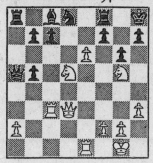

POSITION AFTER WHITE'S 22ND MOVE

With the terrific threat of: 23. Q-Q4 ch.

22.		Kt × P
23.	R × Kt	B × R
24.	Q-Q4 ch.	P-B3

For: 24. . . . K-Kt1. 25. Kt-K7 mate.

| 25. | Kt × KBP | Q-Kt3 |
| 26. | Q-K5 | Q-Q3 |

There is nothing better. The discovered check is immediately fatal.

27. R × P!   Resigns

A charming finish. If: 27. . . . Q × Q. 28. R × RP mate. If: 27. . . . Q × R. 28. Q × Q and Black cannot avoid mate.

Game (3)

Games in which tactics predominate are not easy to analyse and explain unless they happen to be one's own. For this reason, I give below a game I played some years ago with notes based on my ideas and reactions during play.   Although the engagement is convulsive it is hardly adventurous as so much of the play is dictated by necessity. It is an expository example of an active defence.

White	Black
Imré Konig	Dr. Michel
(*Jugoslavia*)	(*Switzerland*)

Prague Team Tournament, 1931

1. P-K4	P-K4
2. Kt-KB3	Kt-QB3
3. B-Kt5	P-QR3

The opening is a Ruy Lopez, Morphy Defence (see Chapter V, Opening (5)).

4. B-R4	Kt-B3
5. O-O	B-K2

Black prefers the more solid line.

6. R-K1	P-QKt4
7. B-Kt3	P-Q3
8. P-QB3	

The apparently strong: 9. P-Q4 fails, on account of: 9. . . . QKt × P.   10. Kt × Kt, P × Kt.   11. Q × P, P-B4; followed by P-B5 winning the bishop.   This is the famous " Noah's Ark " trap, so named because of its antiquity.

8.	QKt-R4
9. B-B2	P-B4
10. P-Q4	Q-B2

Black manages to hold the centre.   This is a well-known position in the Ruy Lopez, the variation beginning: 5. . . . B-K2 being known as Tchigorin's Defence.

11. P-KR3.

The pin would prove embarrassing.

DIAGRAM 95

POSITION AFTER BLACK'S 10TH MOVE

11.	O-O
12. P-QR4	B-Q2
13. B-Kt5	

An investment for the future.

| 13. | KR-B1 |

Threatening to win a pawn by BP × P, as White could not reply P × P because of the inadequately defended bishop on QB2. White is therefore forced to liquidate the centre.

| 14. P × KP | QP × P |
| 15. P × P | |

Originally I had intended to play here: 15. Kt × P at once with the continuation: 15. ... Q × Kt. 16. B × Kt, B × B. 17. Q × B; but it appeared to me that Black got sufficient counter-play with: 17. ... R-Q1. 18. Q-Kt4, P-Kt5. Therefore I concluded it would be wise to first exchange the pawns, leaving, after R-Q1, Q × KtP at my disposal.

| 15. | B × KtP |

To avoid the continuation referred to, Black recaptures with the bishop.

16. Kt-R3

Although Black was able to foil my plan, he did so only at the cost of weakening his Q-side pawns. I now divert my efforts towards exploiting this debility.

16.   B-K1

17. P-QKt3

Necessary, as otherwise Black would play: 17. ... P-B5, "fixing" the QKtP, which would, in consequence, become backward and weak; a target for the black rooks.

17.   KR-Kt1

18. Kt-Q2

I wanted to establish a knight on QB4, where, by its dominating influence, I would be able the more easily to exert pressure on Black's weaknesses—QB4 and QR3.

18.   P-R3

This, and the subsequent moves, constitute an ingenious tactical manoeuvre, the implications of which I had not foreseen.

19 B-R4

A thoughtless move. Better was: 19. B-K3, R-Q1. 20. Q-K2, followed by Kt-B4 with slight superiority.

19.   R-Q1

20. Q-K2

I still hoped to carry out my original plan, but—

20.   Kt-R4!

A fine move, which took me by surprise. Black intends to occupy B5 with the knight, a manoeuvre which would not have been feasible if I had retreated the bishop to K3 instead of to R4.

21. Q × Kt.

To permit the knight to establish itself on B5 would be courting trouble.

21.   R × Kt

Better then: 21. . . . B × B.   22. Kt-B3.

22. B × B   Q × B

23. KR-Q1

The open file had to be contested.

23.   P-B3

Disclosing an attack on the queen.

24. Q-Kt4!

A subtle finesse.   Now if Black doubles rooks: 24. . . .
QR-Q1. 25. R × R, R × R. 26. Q-B8!, with promising
possibilities. Black's next move is therefore virtually
forced.

24.   B-Q2

25. Q-B3

Black appears to have gained a tempo, but in doing so
has been compelled to close the Q-file, forcing an exchange
of rooks.

25.   R × R ch.

26. R × R   B-K3

DIAGRAM 96

POSITION AFTER BLACK'S 26TH MOVE

Just when I believed myself free of entanglements I dis-

covered new threats.   The pawn at Kt3 is attacked, and
it is simple to see that on P-B4, Black would get an overwhelming game by Kt-B3-Q5.   R-Kt1 is met by R-Kt1
without disturbing the balance of the position, and therefore I had to seek a combinative defence to the threat—
an active rather than a passive weapon.

27. Q-K2!

Now after: 27. . . . B × KtP.   28. B × B, Kt × B.
29. Q-B4 ch., Q-B2 (forced, as the knight is *en prise*).
30. R-Q5 regains the pawn with advantage; and after:
27. . . . Kt × P, the problem-like 28. Kt-B4! wins, for
the black knight has no escape square, and: 28. . . . B × Kt
is met by: 29. Q × B ch., followed by B × Kt; whereas
after: 28. . . . R-Kt1, the reply: 29. R-Kt1 leaves Black
again without a move, for 29. . . . Q-B2 is refuted by 30.
R × Kt!

27.   Q-KB2

Now the KtP is again threatened.

28. R-Q6!

Although 28. P-QKt4, P × P.   29. P × P, Kt-B5.   30.
Kt × Kt was perfectly playable, the text move is far more
forceful.

28.   Kt × P

29. R × P   R-Q1

With the unpleasant threat of P-B5 and Kt-B4-Q6.
To meet this line a further combination had to be found.

30. R-Kt6

Now: 30. . . . P-B5 is not playable as I had prepared:
31. Kt × P!, B × Kt.   32. Q × B, Q × Q.   33. B × Kt
with the net gain of a pawn.   Or: 30. . . . R-Q7.   31.
B × Kt, R × Q.   32. B × B wins a piece.

30.   Kt-Q7

31. Q-Kt5.

At last White is able to counter-attack.

31.   P-B5

32. Q-B6.

Threatening, of course, Q × B.

32.   R-K1
33. B-R4   R-K2
34. R-Kt8 ch.   K-R2
35. Q-R8

Hoping for: 36. R-R8 ch., K-Kt3. 37. B-K8 winning the exchange; but better was first: 35. R-Q8 to drive the black knight from its commanding position when White would have had excellent chances.

35.   Q-R4!

The white pieces are far away, and the black queen is able to penetrate the camp.

36. R-R8 ch.   K-Kt3
37. Q-Q8

37. B-K8 ch., B-B2 would have been bad for White. This queen move attacks both rook and knight.

37.   Q-K7

The saving move.

38. Q × R   Q-K8 ch.
39. K-R2   Kt-B8 ch.
40. K-Kt1   Kt-K6 dis. ch.
41. K-R2

Draw by perpetual check. Black has no time to play: 41. . . . Q × KBP (threatening the mate by Q × P) as 42. B-K8 ch. would win; viz: 42. . . . K-Kt4. 43. Q × KtP ch., K-B5 (K-R5. 44. R × P mate). 44. Q × BP ch., B-B4 (K × P loses the queen). 45. Q × RP ch., K × P. 46. B-B6 ch., K-Q6. 47. Q-Q6 ch., K × P. 48 Q × P ch., etc. It is rarely necessary to calculate variations to this length, the position lending itself to a king-hunt, of which the foregoing example is typical. Such chases, unless the king can gain sanctuary, usually have but one result.

Game (4)

This game is a model example of the way to achieve and maintain superiority in the centre. White postpones the advance of the important pawn (in this case the KBP) until he has deprived his opponent of every vestige of counter-play.

White	*Black*
Dr. A. Alekhine	A. Brinkmann

Kecskemet, 1927

1. P-K4	P-K4
2. Kt-KB3	Kt-QB3
3. B-Kt5	P-Q3

With the advances made in opening theory it is now considered best to play first: 3. . . . Kt-B3; and after: 4. O-O, P-Q3. 5. P-Q4, B-Q2. 6. Kt-B3, B-K2. 7. B × Kt, B × B. 8. Q-Q3, Kt-Q2!. 9. B-K3, P × P. (White threatened: 10. P-Q5). 10. B × P, O-O. 11. Kt-Q5, B-B3 (Maroczy—Capablanca, London, 1922). Black was able to relieve his position by exchanges.

4. P-Q4	B-Q2
5. Kt-B3	Kt-B3
6. B × Kt	B × B
7. Q-Q3	

White is threatening: 8. P × P as his KP is now twice defended.

7.	P × P

Now Black cannot carry out the simplifying line suggested above, as after: 7. . . . Kt-Q2. 8. B-K3 (Black can now meet: 8. P-Q5 with Kt-B4!, attacking the queen and providing an escape square for the bishop), P × P. 9. B × P, the KB cannot be developed (on account of B × P) and he must surrender the centre under unfavourable circumstances.

8. Kt × P   P-KKt3
9. B-Kt5!

This text move is now considered better than: 9. Kt × B, P × Kt. 10. Q-R6, Q-Q2. 11. Q-Kt7, R-B1. 12. Q × RP, B-Kt2 (Nimzowitsch—Capablanca, St. Petersburg, 1914), when Black obtained pressure on the Q-side for the lost pawn.

9.   B-Kt2
10. O-O-O.

White castles Q-side, thereby obtaining two major pieces on the Q-file. This move also prevents Black castling K-side, as after: 10. . . . O-O?. 11. Kt × B, P × Kt. 12. P-K5, P × P. 13. Q × Q, QR × Q. 14. R × R, R × R. 15. Kt-K4! would win the exchange.

10.   Q-Q2

10. . . . Q-B1 was to be preferred, leaving the Q2 square for the knight.

11. P-KR3!

Restricting the action of the knight.

11.   O-O
12. KR-K1   KR-K1

This deprives the knight of a square to which to retreat. For this reason: 12. . . . K-R1 was better.

13. Q-B3   Kt-R4
14. P-KKt4   B × Kt
15. R × B   Kt-Kt2

By this little manoeuvre Black succeeds in finding employment for the knight; but now his pawn structure

on the K-side is enfeebled by the absence of the complementary bishop (Chapter VI, Diagram 67).

16. B-B6

Black was threatening: 16. . . . Kt-K3, winning the
exchange.

16.   R-K3

The position has now crystallised to some extent.
White firmly holds the centre, and in addition has effectively undermined the black king position.   It is instructive to see how Alekhine utilizes his advantages.

17. R(4)-Q1

To retain the bishop on the diagonal.

17.   Kt-K1
18. B-Q4   Q-K2
19. R-K3   Kt-Kt2
20. Q-B4   Q-R5!

A necessary precaution as White was preparing to open
the KR-file with: 21. Q-R6 and 27. P-KR4, etc.

21. R(1)-K1   R(1)-K1

DIAGRAM 97

POSITION AFTER BLACK'S 21ST MOVE

The position now reached is worth examining as it is

a type which often recurs. White is in possession of the centre, and has successfully prevented Black from playing either of the freeing moves P-Q4 and P-KB4. He will initiate his attack with P-KB4, but he first consolidates on the Q-side as this is the only quarter in which Black might be able to obtain a measure of counter-play.

22.	P-Kt3	P-QR4
23.	P-QR4	P-Kt3
24.	K-Kt2	R(1)-K2
25.	Q-R2	

Preparing P-B4

25.		Kt-K1
26.	P-B4	Kt-B3

Black hopes to gain a vital tempo by the double threat of Kt × KP and Kt × KtP.

27. P-B5!

But White has the answer prepared. Now: 27. . . . Kt × KtP would provoke: 28. Q-B4! and 27. . . . Kt × KP, of course 28. P × R.

27.		R × P
28.	Kt × R	Kt × Kt
29.	Q-B4	P-KKt4

If: 29. . . . P-Q4. 30. P × P, RP × P. 31. B-B6 wins as both the queen and rook are attacked.

30.	Q-B1	P-Q4

The knight is pinned. If now: 30. . . . Kt-Q7. 31. R × R, Kt × Q. 32. R-K8 ch., B × R. 33. R × B mate.

31. P-B4

White strikes at the support.

31.		Q-R3
32.	P-B6	R-K1
33.	P × P	B × P
34.	Q-B5	Resigns

As White, already the exchange to the good, must now come out a whole piece ahead, while Black is unable to adjust the material balance by " pawn hunting " on account of the mate threat; viz: 34. ... B-R1. 35. R × Kt, B × R.   36. R × B, R × R.   37. Q × R, Q × RP??. 38. Q-K8 (or R8) mate.

Game (5)

An encore for the star performer.   In this game Dr. Alekhine demonstrates the importance of a single diagonal in an apparently balanced struggle.

	White	*Black*
	Dr. A. Alekhine	K. Junge
	Played in 1942	
1.	P-K4	P-K4
2.	Kt-KB3	Kt-QB3
3.	B-Kt5	P-QR3
4.	B-R4	Kt-B3
5.	O-O	B-K2
6.	Q-K2	

The " Worrall Attack ".   In Game (3) I played R-K1 here: it is all a matter of choice.   The text-move heralds a lively game.

6.		P-QKt4
7.	B-Kt3	O-O
8.	P-B3	P-Q4

An enterprising move which could lead to interesting play after: 9. P × P, P-K5 !.   10. P × Kt, B-KKt5 and Black obtains a strong attack.

9. P-Q3

Black is now forced to declare his intentions as this move threatens to win a pawn by: 10. P × P, Kt × P.

11. Kt × P

9.	P × P

A strategical error. Black opens the Q-file which White is able to occupy with his rook. Better was: 9. . . . P-Q5. 10. P × P, Kt × QP. 11. Kt × Kt, Q × Kt. 12. B-K3, Q-Q3. 13. Kt-B3 (or better, R-B1), B-K3. 14. B × B, P × B! 15. P-B4, P × P. 16. B × P, P-K4. 17. B-Kt3, QR-Q1, with about equal chances (Kerés—Dr. Euwe, The Hague, 1948).

10. P × P	B-KKt5
11. P-KR3	B-R4
12. B-Kt5!	

Alekhine finds the weak point in his opponent's position. This move, which looks just like an ordinary developing move, has a two-fold purpose; in the first place it prevents: 12. . . . Kt-QR4 (it is Black's aim to drive the white KB off the powerful diagonal) because of: 13. P-Kt4, Kt × B. 14. P × Kt, B-Kt3. 15. Kt × P, B × P. (15. . . . . Kt × KP. 16 Kt-B6). 16 B × Kt, P × B. 17. Q × B, P × Kt. 18. Q × KP with the win of a pawn. Secondly, it threatens: 13. B × Kt, B × B. 14. B-Q5, followed by P-QR4 with pressure on the white squares.

12.	Kt-K1
13. B × B	B × Kt

Forced, since on: 13. . . . Q × B. 14. B-Q5, Q-Q3. 15. P-KKt4, B-Kt3. 16. Kt × P. And on: 13. . . . . Kt × B. 14. P-Kt4, B-Kt3. 15. Kt × P.

14. Q × B	Kt × B
15. R-Q1	Kt-Q3
16. Kt-Q2	P-B3

We have now arrived at the second stage of the game. White has secured the superior position thanks to his

finer strategy, his advantage lying in the strength of his
well-posted bishop and the greater freedom possessed by
his KR. Black has prepared a slow line, of which his
last move is indicative. He would have been well advised
to have considered a more active defence; for example:
16. ... K-R1. 17. Kt-B1, P-KB4.

17. Kt-B1   Q-B2
18. P-QR4   QR-Q1

It is dangerous to leave White with control of the
QR-file; but the retention of the rook on R1 also had its
hazards, for after: 19. P × P, RP × P (otherwise the RP
is backward and the square Q4 passes to White's control).
20. R × R, R × R; the important square KB2 would
have been weakened.

19. Kt-Kt3   Kt(2)-B1
20. P × P   RP × P

21. Kt-B5!

Much stronger than the alternative: 21. Kt-R5, Q-K2.
22. R-R6, P-Kt3; and the knight would have to retreat
(23. Kt-B6 ch., K-Kt2).

21.   Kt-Kt3
22. Q-K3!   Kt × Kt

On: 22. ... Kt(Kt3)-B5, White would have had the
disagreeable reply: 23. B × Kt, Kt × B. 24. Q-B5!, with
diverse threats, as: 25. R × R, R × R. 26. Q × BP or
26. R-R7

23. P × Kt

It is true that White has now doubled pawns, but his
assets far outweigh his liabilities.

23.   P-B4

Not: 23. ... Kt-Q4. 24. Q-B3, Kt-B3. 25. P-Kt4,
with a strong attack.

24. P-B6

A correct pawn sacrifice.

24.   P × P

25. Q-R6.   P-B4

DIAGRAM 98

POSITION AFTER BLACK'S 25TH MOVE

To meet the threat: 26. B-B2.

26. B × P ch!

A fine conclusion! Black can retake the bishop with no less than three pieces.

26.   Q × B

If: 26. . . . K × B?. 27. Q × P ch. wins the queen—the " through check ". If: 26. . . . R × B. 27. Q-Kt5 ch., followed by R × R, and if: 26. . . . K-R1. 27. Q-B6 mate.

27. R × R   Kt-R5

If: 27. . . . R × R, then: 28. Q-Kt5 ch., etc.

28. P-QKt3   Resigns

For after: 28. . . . Kt × P. 29. QR-R8 wins quickly. There is nothing to be done.

The white bishop dominated the game throughout, and

it was therefore fitting that it should administer the coup-de-grace. Note how, although thrice defended, that anatomical weakness at KB2 was once again the cause of a collapse.

Game (6)

Our last game is concerned primarily with strategical considerations. It is a good example of a centre-pawn formation reduced to immobility, and consequent impotence, by clever positional play.

White	Black
Sir G. A. Thomas	J. R. Capablanca

Margate, 1936

1.	P-Q4	Kt-KB3
2.	P-QB4	P-K3
3.	Kt-QB3	P-Q4

This is, of course, a Queen's Gambit by transposition of moves.

4.	B-Kt5	B-K2
5.	P-K3	O-O
6.	Kt-B3	QKt-Q2
7.	R-B1	P-B3

All very orderly !

8.	B-Q3	P-KR3
9.	B-R4	

This is the normal position in the Orthodox Defence, which gives Black a solid, but rather cramped game. Every opening, we know, presents some sort of problem for the defender, and here it is clearly the development of the QB, which explains Black's next three moves.

9.		P × P
10.	B × P	P-QKt4

11. B-Q3   P-R3

12. O-O

White should have attempted to frustrate Black in his
designs. More aggressive, therefore, was: 12. P-QR4
immediately, when after: 12. ... P × P (12. ... P-Kt5.
13. B × Kt, Kt × B. 14. Kt-K4! prevents Black playing
P-QB4). 13. Kt × P, Q-R4 ch. 14. Kt-Q2, B-Kt5.
15. Kt-B3, P-B4. 16. Kt-Kt3 (note how the two knights
work in conjunction, one unpinning the other), Q-Kt3.
17. P × P, B × P. 18. Kt × B, Q × Kt; with an approximately equal game.

12.   P-B4

13. P-R4   P-B5

14. B-K2

White selects the wrong plan. He intends to attack
the pawn chain, and possibly to dislocate it by P-QKt3
at an early stage; but his best chances lay on the K-side,
and he should have kept the bishop on the Kt1-R7
diagonal; viz: 14. B-Kt1, Kt-Q4. 15. B × B, Q × B.
16. P-QKt3. QKt-Kt3. 17. P × BP. Now Black gets
a stranglehold on the centre.

14.   Kt-Q4

15. B × B   Q × B

16. Q-Q2   B-Kt2

White could not have advanced at once: 16. P-K4, as
16. ... Kt-B5 would have proved very strong. Now his
hopes of advancing the KP vanish, for after: 17. P-K4,
Kt × Kt. 18. Q × Kt, B × P wins a pawn; instead
he presents Black with an open R-file.

17. P × P   Kt × Kt

18. Q × Kt   P × P

19. R-R1.   KR-B1

Now the disadvantage of White's 14th move is apparent;
the black bishop restraining the centre pawns effectively,
allowing Black's Q-side majority to become menacing.

20. KR-B1   Kt-Kt3

Black is in no hurry, and first cements his position.

21. Kt-K1   P-B4

22. B-B3   B-Q4

23. Q-B2   Q-B3

Black prevents White playing P-K4 by exerting pressure
on the QP

24. Q-Q2   Q-B1

Preparing P-Kt5

25. Kt-B2   B × B

26. P × B   Kt-Q4

DIAGRAM 99

POSITION AFTER BLACK'S 26TH MOVE.

The overture to a typical Capablanca combination.
Black now permits P-K4, as he sees that he can exploit
the attenuated K-side. Note how neither side will

exchange rooks, for this would permit the other to occupy the open file. This configuration is frequently encountered.

27.	P-K4	P × P
28.	P × P	Q-B5!

Much stronger than posting the knight on this square, when White has a plausible defence in: 29. . . . Kt-K1. Now White cannot play: 29. Q × Q, as after: 29. . . . Kt × Q; the double threat of Kt-K7 ch. (winning the exchange) and Kt-Q6 (with a crushing position) would decide.

29.	Q-K2	Q-Kt4 ch.
30.	K-R1	Kt-B5
31.	Q-B3	

31. . . . Q-Kt7 mate was threatened.

31.		Kt-Q6
32.	R-KKt1	R × R

Black exchanges at the right moment.

33.	R × R	Q-Q7

And White resigned, for there is no defence to: 34. . . . R-KB1, when mate, or ruinous loss of material would follow swiftly.

A sound and logical game, conducted in Capablanca's inimitable style.

CHAPTER IX

GENERAL INFORMATION

This short chapter, in dealing with extraneous matters, ignores the title and the intention of the book.

A background of general information is wholly desirable in any game however, and this is considered sufficient excuse for its inclusion.

Match Play

The first and paramount rule to remember in match play is that a chessman once touched must be moved; and that once a man is played (the move is completed on letting go of the man) the move stands.

It is a very good idea to keep to this rule in friendly games; there is nothing more annoying in chess than the player who dithers when making a move. Decide on your move, execute it incisively, withdraw your hand.

If you get the opportunity, watch a good player. You will not see him pick up a piece and wave it in a series of concentric circles before banging it down on a square only to retract it a moment later.

If an opposing chessman is touched, the rule is that it must be captured if this is legitimately possible. If it is desired to centralize a man that has become misplaced, this can be done by saying " *j'adoube* " (Fr. " I adjust ") before touching the man in question, and then only when it is your turn to move.

Matches and tournaments are decided on points—one point is accorded for a win, half a point for a draw.

In match play a time limit is normally imposed on the number of moves each player shall make in a prescribed period. Twenty to twenty-four moves an hour is usual, and if this time, which is allowed to each player (who is also permitted to think in his opponent's time) is exceeded, the player overstepping the time limit is ruled to have lost the game. A few chess-players consider it unsporting to win in this fashion; why is not clear, since the laws of chess are as firm on this point as any other.

In order to record the time taken by each player a chess clock is used. This instrument consists of two ordinary clocks side by side connected by a lever which, when depressed, stops the clock on the one side and restarts it on the other; hence the two clocks never run simultaneously.

When a player has made his move, he presses his lever, thereby stopping his clock and setting his opponent's in motion. Should he omit to do this, his opponent will be thinking " free of charge " as it were in his (the first player's) time.

Chess clocks have two small strips of metal, known as flags, fixed to the dials. They are so positioned that when the minute hand approaches the hour, it will push the flag up, releasing it exactly as the hour is passed, thereby eliminating any dispute that might otherwise have arisen as to whether or not the time limit had been exceeded.

Not all games may be concluded at the end of a match, when one of two courses is normally adopted:

(a) The game may be adjudicated (i.e., the result agreed upon) on the spot by the respective match captains, or by a strong player or players nominated by them. Sometimes the game may be forwarded to an acknowledged expert. Adjudications are common in team matches.

(b) The game may be adjourned, the players resuming when convenient. The procedure at adjournment is for the player whose turn it is to move to write his move down without making it on the board and without disclosing it. The clocks are then stopped and the game position, together with the clock times and the sealed move (often all on the one piece of paper) are put in an envelope. The envelope is sealed and the player who made the sealed move signs across the flap. The envelope is then given to the tournament director or to the second player to retain until the game is restarted. All illegal sealed move forfeits the game.

Players are permitted to analyse adjourned games. It is common practice but dubious ethics to seek advice at this stage.

Is it an advantage or a disadvantage to seal the move? It's an open question. The player who has sealed the move can of course analyse the position one move ahead of his opponent. This may be a big advantage if there were a number of plausible moves available as the second player will be obliged to examine a number of irrelevant lines. However, if the sealed move was not the best then it is likely that the second player, who has been able to study the position in depth, will take advantage of the lapse.

Etiquette

It is not permitted in any way to disturb or distract a player during a game. In practice, this rule may prove difficult to interpret but in general it can be said that the player who is distracted is the best judge of what is to him a distraction.

A player who resigns a game should obviously do so gracefully. Poor sportsmanship is unfortunately to be found in chess as it is in other games; one famous player wryly remarked that he had never won a game off a fit opponent!

Spectators should never pass audible comment on any match game in progress and nor should they interfere in any such game even if a breach of the rules has been committed.

Chess Clubs and British Chess

Chess clubs in Great Britain may broadly be divided into two groups—those that are chess clubs pure and simple and those that are sections of other clubs such as works' clubs, social clubs and the like. The bulk of the active players probably belong in the second category, but the stronger players are mostly to be found in the first group.

Chess clubs usually meet one or two evenings a week and apart from affording the opportunity for friendly games, offer various activities such as tournaments, matches against other clubs, etc. Most chess clubs are affiliated to their respective County Associations which in turn are affiliated to one or other of the regional Unions. These Unions, together with a few other independent bodies, send delegates to the British Chess Federation which is responsible for organised chess on a national basis.

It is a good thing to join a chess club as soon as possible, preferably one of the less well-known ones where the standard of play is not high and the newcomer may soon have the pleasure of winning a game or two. A pleasing feature of chess life is that the traveller or holiday-maker is likely to find himself welcome as a guest at the local club during his stay, and this applies equally abroad as at home.

Congresses

A feature of chess since the war has been the rise in popularity of the congress. A chess congress is an open tournament (usually a number of tournaments) covering anything from a week-end to a fortnight. Congresses are often arranged at resorts so that the competitor combines chess with a holiday. Normally one game is played each day, but more are played in week-end events which are often a test of stamina as well as ability.

Literature

Thousands of books have been written about chess, covering the game in all its aspects. Most public libraries now offer a fair selection, but the average player will wish to have for his own use at least one book on the openings and one on the end-game. These two books will be used mainly for reference and are really essential for anyone who aspires to match or tournament play.

Two leading periodicals published in Great Britain are the *British Chess Magazine* and *Chess*. There are a number of other publications as well as many scores of newspaper columns devoted to the game.

Famous Players

It is invidious to attempt this subject in a paragraph, but some players are so widely known, if only by name, even among non-players, that these at least deserve a mention.

Capablanca and Alekhine were two former world champions (and great rivals) who are represented in the

Games Section (Chapter VIII). An American, Paul Morphy, who had a brief and meteoric career in the middle of the last century and had no equal in his day is well-remembered by the romantics, but Steinitz, an Austrian, probably contributed more to chess theory than any other player before or since.

The decline of Russian dominance of the International scene began with the rise of Bobby Fischer and Britain can now boast two Grandmasters in Tony Miles and Ray Keene.

Simultaneous Chess

Simultaneous displays are a feature of many clubs' activities. A master opposes a number of players (usually around twenty) at the same time.

Each player sits at a board with the black pieces, the expert playing with the white pieces in every case.

The solo player then walks round the tables (the sets are arranged in a semi-circle or in two lines) and makes his opening move on each board. Each player withholds his reply until the simultaneous player comes round again to his board. The master then moves again and immediately goes on to the next board. Displays of this nature take from about two to four hours the master normally winning a half to two-thirds of the games, conceding one or two and drawing the remainder.

Time is heavily on the side of the challengers to begin with but this advantage is gradually reduced as the number of unfinished games diminishes.

Blindfold Chess

Many strong players are able to conduct one or more games without sight of the board. Moves are announced, and the blindfold player may or may not be literally blindfolded. The world record is over forty games played simultaneously in this fashion—an incredible achievement.

Correspondence Chess

Playing chess by post is popular among those who have time to spare or who are inhibited by domicile or infirmity from taking part in over-the-board activities. A correspondence game may last a few months or a few years and is a good way of improving one's powers of analysis.

There are many correspondence chess organisations, both national and international, and a player may of course participate in several matches and tournaments at the same time.

Chess Problems

A large number of newspapers print in their columns a regular chess problem above a legend which runs "White mates in two" or "White mates in three".

The position given is frequently quixotic, and one in which White is usually possessed of a heavy preponderance of material; which has caused some chess-players to dismiss problems as unworthy of their consideration.

Chess problems, however, are as removed from chess as crossword puzzles are from literature.

In chess, the object of the game is to defeat the opponent, the means by which this end is achieved, or the time it takes, being unimportant. In problems, however, the opponent is represented by time. Mate must be effected within the stipulated number of moves. Problemists maintain that the game involves too much laborious and profitless woodshifting; that the artistry of fifty games can be compounded into a single artificial position.

Fairy Chess

Fairy chess covers in a general sense all those divertissements which are related to but deviate from the normal game. In this sense, the games mentioned in the following paragraph are Fairy chess. The term however is more commonly applied to problems. The artistic expression of the orthodox composer is severally constrained by the confines of the chessboard, the limitations of the regular chessmen and the rules of play.

In Fairy chess, the composer makes his own conditions. These may include the use of a different board, different men and different rules—sometimes all three in the same problem. Some wonderful work has been done in this field.

Other Games with the Chessmen

There are many digressive games possible with the normal chessmen.

Kriegspiel, Losing Game, Progressive Chess, Rifle Chess, Cylinder Chess—these are but a few. They are occasionally played in clubs but have no regular following and are outside the scope of this book.

Forsyth Notation

For taking down a position the Forsyth notation is unexcelled. Facing the board from White's side, squares and men are enumerated, starting at the top left-hand corner (Black's QR1) and working from left to right, rank by rank. White men are given in capitals, black in small letters.

The position in Diagram 9 (page 30) would this be recorded: r3k2r/ (black rook, three squares, black king, two squares, black rook) pp5p/ (black pawn, black pawn, five squares, black pawn) 1P1Bkt1p1/ (one square, white pawn, one square, white bishop, black knight, one square black pawn, one square)

2pP4/1R6/1kt3P2/P2p1KPP/1R3B2.

Algebraic

The algebraic or continental notation differs basically from the English system in that each square has but a single description. White's QR square as the cornerstone files are lettered from left to right, a-h and ranks numbered progressively up the board, 1-8. A square is denominated by the combination of the file-letter (written first) and rank number. White's QR1 is therefore written "a1", Black's QR1 "a8".

Here the essential division between the algebraic and the English system is apparent; in the English, the square a1 would be QR1 or QR8, according to the player's standpoint; in the algebraic it has only the one description.

The pieces are referred to by letters, as in the English notation, but the hyphen ("to") is omitted. A pawn move takes no initial letter.

Ba4 is the same as B-QR4 if a White move (note also that in the algebraic no confusion exists as to which side of the board the move is made). The symbol a4 denotes P-QR4 if a White move, P-QR5 if a Black move.

The distinguishing cross (×) for a capture is common to both systems, but in the continental the square on which the capture is made is recorded, and not the symbol for the captured man. The initial P (pawn) is employed if it is the unit making the capture.

Thus in the algebraic system a white move P × a4 signifies pawn (which must clearly be on b3) takes the

black man (whatever it may be) on a4 (QR4- Black's QR5).
Notice the complete absence of ambiguity.

DIAGRAM 100

THE ALGEBRAIC NOTATION

Where confusion might ensue, the file letter or rank
number is inserted. The White move R(4) × Kt would
be expressed R(4) × b3. The move P(R3) × Kt as
simply P × b3, no duplication existing with P(Q5) × Kt
(P × e6).

International Chess

The Fédération Internationale des Échecs (F.I.D.E.)
is the recognised world body responsible, *inter alia*, for
the World Championship and Chess Olympiad arrange-
ments. Nearly all countries where chess is organised are
members of F.I.D.E.

Master Titles

Grandmaster and International Master titles are conferred by F.I.D.E. from time to time on players whose performance in international events reached the required standard. Titles below this level (e.g., National Master, Candidate Master) are awarded by national chess authorities and vary from country to country. Only very strong players ever achieve recognition in this way.

Grading

Many countries now grade players who compete regularly in approved matches and tournaments and who attain a certain minimum standard.

A player's rating, or grading as it is commonly called, is derived from the aggregate of his results over a period, the strength of his opponents being taken into account.

The grading list is used to determine qualification for national titles and, more widely, to assist in selection of players for matches and tournaments. It is also an incentive to the individual.

Other Notations

There are international codes for use in correspondence, radio, cable and telephone matches. Two letters or figures denote each square on the board, and a move is transmitted as a four-symbol group, the first two symbols indicating the square on which the man to be moved stands, the second two symbols the square to which it is to be moved. Checks and captures are not annotated.

INDEX

OUR PUBLISHING POLICY

HOW WE CHOOSE

Our policy is to consider every deserving manuscript and we can give special editorial help where an author is an authority on his subject but an inexperienced writer. We are rigorously selective in the choice of books we publish. We set the highest standards of editorial quality and accuracy. This means that a *Paperfront* is easy to understand and delightful to read. Where illustrations are necessary to convey points of detail, these are drawn up by a subject specialist artist from our panel.

HOW WE KEEP PRICES LOW

We aim for the big seller. This enables us to order enormous print runs and achieve the lowest price for you. Unfortunately, this means that you will not find in the *Paperfront* list any titles on obscure subjects of minority interest only. These could not be printed in large enough quantities to be sold for the low price at which we offer this series.

We sell almost all our *Paperfronts* at the same unit price. This saves a lot of fiddling about in our clerical departments and helps us to give you world-beating value. Under this system, the longer titles are offered at a price which we believe to be unmatched by any publisher in the world.

OUR DISTRIBUTION SYSTEM

Because of the competitive price, and the rapid turnover, *Paperfronts* are possibly the most profitable line a bookseller can handle. They are stocked by the best bookshops all over the world. It may be that your bookseller has run out of stock of a particular title. If so, he can order more from us at any time – we have a fine reputation for "same day" despatch, and we supply any order, however small (even a single copy), to any bookseller who has an account with us. We prefer you to buy from your bookseller, as this reminds him of the strong underlying public demand for *Paperfronts*. Members of the public who live in remote places, or who are housebound, or whose local bookseller is unco-operative, can order direct from us by post.

FREE

If you would like an up-to-date list of all paperfront titles currently available, send a stamped self-addressed envelope to
ELLIOT RIGHT WAY BOOKS, BRIGHTON RD.,
LOWER KINGSWOOD, SURREY, U.K.